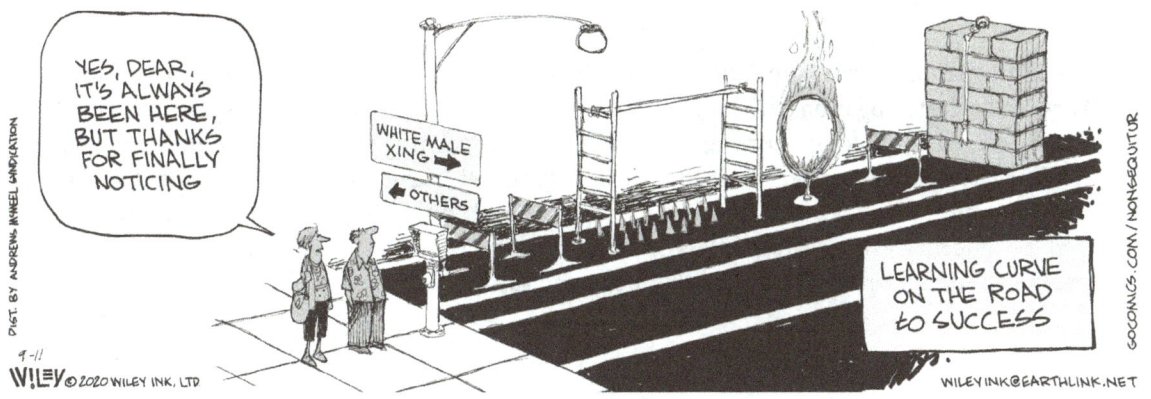

NON SEQUITUR ©2020 Wiley Ink, Inc. Dist. By ANDREWS MCMEEL SYNDICATION. Reprinted with permission. All rights reserved.

Praise for this book

Peter Smith combines Studs Terkel's storytelling about the meaningfulness of work with motivation and support reminiscent of Gail Sheehy in *Stories from the Education Underground.* He lets readers know that they can control their destiny by being true to their skills and passions.

Anthony Carnevale
Research Professor and Director, Georgetown Center for Education and Work

◆ ◆ ◆

Through the compelling life stories of individuals who successfully overcame obstacles to educational and economic opportunity, Peter Smith captures the talent and capacity that colleges and employers too often ignore. *Stories from the Educational Underground: The New Frontier for Learning and Work* is a must-read for those of us in the world of learning and work who strive to deliver on America's promise of educational and economic opportunity for all.

Mildred García, Ed.D.
President/CEO, American Association of State Colleges and Universities

◆ ◆ ◆

In this fantastic book, Peter Smith takes us behind the data regarding underserved adult learners, allowing them to tell their incredibly inspirational stories of lessons learned in and, mostly, out of school. Smith's argument is that "we need to bring personal learning from the margins to the mainstream of American life." He is right, and the time is right ... for action!

Ted Mitchell
CEO, The American Council on Education

Contributed by Anthony Carnevale, Mildred Garcia and Theodore R. Mitchell. © Kendall Hunt Publishing Company

◆ ◆ ◆

Peter Smith: *Stories from the Education Underground: The New Frontier for Learning and Work* is a deft interrogation of the inequitable way our education and training system ascribes value to learning. Through contrasting his privileged learning journey through Princeton and Harvard with the experiences of a diverse group of learners who lacked benefit social and economic advantage, Smith makes a passionate and compelling argument for the urgent need to value all learning—regardless of where it happens—as a strategy for social justice. A timely and thought-provoking read that points towards a more equitable future.

Michael Collins
Vice President, Jobs for the Future

◆ ◆ ◆

Peter Smith and a chorus of voices call us to remember an equity essential: Everyone deserves the opportunity to thrive. As we grow along our winding life paths, many of us need more than one shot at success. Skills are developed from diverse experiences, and the world's next great talent may come from somewhere you never expected. Open your mind and beliefs with these stories of blind corners, long odds, and "in-spite-of" successes.

Wendi Copeland
Chief Strategic Partnership Activation Officer,
Goodwill Industries International

◆ ◆ ◆

"The assault on democracy, the urgent need to reskill and upskill millions of American workers, and the inequities of social justice further revealed by the pandemic have brought us to an inflection point. They require education and business leaders to reimagine the workforce for the future of work and the good of the country. Let's begin that journey by taking a leadership role in restoring the "Soul of America." Let's occupy and settle *The New Frontier for Learning and Work*!"

Dr. Rufus Glasper
CEO, The League for Innovation in the Community College

◆ ◆ ◆

The march towards educational equity begins with valuing the deeply personal lived experiences of all learners. Peter Smith's timely examination of the 'hidden credentials' earned outside of traditional institutional models serves as a clarion call for everyone who cares about economic mobility in this country.

Dr. Courtney Hills McBeth
Vice President, Strada

Contributed by Michael Collins, Wendi Copeland and Dr. Rufus Glasper. © Kendall Hunt Publishing Company. © Dr. Courtney Hills McBeth. Reprinted by permission.

Stories from the
Educational Underground

The New Frontier for Learning and Work

Dr. Peter Smith

Cover image: © Shutterstock.com
Contributed by Jane Oates. © Kendall Hunt Publishing Company
Contributed by Gregory Fowler. © Kendall Hunt Publishing Company

www.kendallhunt.com
Send all inquiries to:
4050 Westmark Drive
Dubuque, IA 52004-1840

Copyright © 2021 by Kendall Hunt Publishing Company

ISBN 978-1-7924-7293-0

All rights reserved. No part of this publication may be reproduced, stored in a retrieval system, or transmitted, in any form or by any means, electronic, mechanical, photocopying, recording, or otherwise, without the prior written permission of the copyright owner.

Published in the United States of America

Contents

Foreword – Dr. Rufus Glasper, CEO, League for Innovation in the Community College xi

Introduction 1

Section 1: My Story 11

Section 2: The Learning Journey 23

    The Merry-Go-Round 24

        Rashaan Green 25

        Dinesha Monteiro 29

        Susan Fenwick 33

    Dreams Deferred: One Step at a Time 38

        Susan Johnson 39

        Sarah Aronack 45

        Heather Lumsden 49

        Kalimah Shabazz 52

    On Their Own Terms: Self-Directed Learners 56

        Samuel Muraguri 57

        Chris Wilson 61

        Rahim Fazal 65

        Michelle Daniels 70

Section 3: Bridges to the Future 75

   People and Programs 76

      Katie Reigelsperger 77

      Calvin Duker 83

      Jim Clemens 88

      Ron Williams 92

   Colleges That Helped 97

      Jose Rodriguez 98

      Anna Raymond.. 102

      Andrew Wheatley 105

      Betty Graham 109

Section 4: The Capstone—Michael's Story 115

Conclusion 127

Afterword – Louis Soares, Chief Learning and Innovation Officer,
          American Council on Education 133

Appendix 141

   Under Ground Programs – Emerging Pathways for
   Learning and Work 141

      New College models 141

          – College UnBound 142

          – SV Academy 142

          – The Community College of Vermont 142

          – Purdue Global University 142

- University of Maryland Global Campus 142
- Western Governors University 142
- Colorado Technical University 142
- Bellevue University 142

Workplace-Based models 142
- Goodwill Industries 143
- McDonald's Archways to Opportunity 143
- Walmart Live Better U 143
- Amazon Career Choice Program 143

Bridging Services 143
- StraighterLine 144
- Credly 144
- Guild 144
- Year Up 144
- College Promise 144

Validation of Personal Learning– Giving Credit Where Credit Is Due 145
- CAEL 145
- American Council of Education 145
- Straighterline 145
- Western Governors University 145
- University of Maryland Global Campus 145
- College UnBound 145
- *Cashing In: How to Get Real Value from Your Lifelong Learning* 145

Contents   vii

GPS for learning and work 145
- eMSI 146
- BurningGlass 146
- The Open Skills Network 146
- Strada 146

Acknowledgments

There are so many people to thank for their help in getting *Stories from the Educational Underground* into print that I almost don't know where to begin. My wife and partner in life, Letitia Chambers, has cast her keen educator's and editor's eye over the manuscript several times. And the result is a far more coherent and readable book. The people who agreed to be interviewed showed extraordinary courage and candor as they shared their life stories and, in so doing, clarified the obstacles they faced and the price they paid on the way to securing opportunity. And finally, the people who helped me find the interview subjects and the organizations for which they work are significant players in this script. All are mentioned, one way or the other, in the text and the Appendices. But my thanks and gratitude to all who contributed are as deep as they are profound. Thank you.

Foreword

By Rufus Glasper
CEO, League for Innovation in the Community College

To be perfectly candid, Peter Smith's *Stories from the Educational Underground* that link personal learning to economic opportunity resonates with my personal life experience. As I read the life stories throughout the book, I was reminded of my own life choices, my youth, and growing up with siblings where four out of seven took the "underground" path. Four of my brothers did not take the collegiate path. Their learning was personal, but they never were able to capitalize on the value of the learning derived from their lived experience or the resulting knowledge of self and society. This book serves as a beacon for the value of recognizing and constructing one's personal capacity. Thanks for the societal reminder of the value which every individual has to contribute!

While they are the stories of just a few people, the lived experiences captured in these interviews represent most students, adults, and senior citizens. Most people are seeking a better life, but many are unaware of how to get there, of how to convert their talent, their accomplishments, and their prior learning into real value.

On the one hand, Peter Smith openly and candidly shares that, for the most part, his ascension in life was influenced, guided, and supported by family members and close acquaintances, and by privilege. They provided guidance and, in some cases, shepherded his early journey in life. He acknowledges that there were supports and guideposts that were available to help him all along his path.

On the other hand, the path many take in life is not like Peter's. It is not dictated positively by the family into which we were born or status in life, including education, job, and wealth. For many of us, it is a search that converts the unknown into a path forward. Put bluntly, similar guideposts are not equally available or used by many first-generation, low-income, or people of color. Ultimately, we are all looking for much the same things: education, work success, family support, and a livable wage. But the paths to career and life success, including the value of and path to college, are not clear. As a result, the choices of how to proceed are muddled at best. And when we get into the real world, we're often routed in different, random directions, with many people going off the formalized educational path, never to return.

Here's a little more about my life story. I am a baby boomer, born in Chicago. Both of my parents worked in the stockyards in a meatpacking plant before the birth of my older brother and me. Upon our births, our mother became a stay-at-home mom. My father did not complete high school but wanted more for his family. So, within a few years, he accepted

Contributed by Dr. Rufus Glasper. © Kendall Hunt Publishing Company a job at the Wisconsin Steel Mill as an apprentice welder with dreams of one day owning a home and working independently. When I was seven, our family moved to a new home in the south suburbs. And two years later, the family had grown to nine with seven children—six boys and the youngest a girl.

Segregation, while patchwork, was a fact of life. We grew up in the Black community of the town, where the city officials denied Black residents access to the public pool. While integrated elementary and junior high schools were allowed, segregated freshman and sophomore high schools existed in separate communities. So, while school board policy permitted integrated sports teams at each grade level, the daily instruction and education through middle school were community-based. However, upon reaching junior year status, all classes and sports integrated. Weird, but very real.

My parents were a real team. They used all their talent to become successful for us all. Over the years, my father started his own business, Glasper and Son's Janitorial Service, and stopped welding. Simultaneously, because he always wanted to be a policeman, he was the first African American to become an auxiliary and then part-time policeman in our city. My mother remained at home. But she also went to our local community college to learn bookkeeping for the new family business. I enjoyed math in high school and used these skills to help my mother keep the financial records. I continued to play football and, when I graduated, I used those skills in addition to my financial experience to make my college selection.

My parents and I chose a small liberal arts college in Iowa. The goal was to focus on getting a degree in Business and Education, to not incur college debt, and to graduate on time. There were 50 African Americans out of a student body of 2100. I immediately became aware that I was no longer in the Chicago area. Some of the college faculty and fellow white students had never experienced Black people, their culture, or their lived experiences including education, resilience, ability to adapt, and success. So, the overall experience was mixed, to put it mildly.

During my first year, I played football and lived in a dorm with a white football player and classmate. Together, we attended a few classes, we studied together, and twice, upon receiving our initial grades from assignments, we compared. He received an A while I received a C. The professor informed me that she did not believe that I actually understood the answers to my class assignment. The basis for her judgment was that because I was Black, born, raised, and educated in the Chicago area, my education was inferior to that of the white students!

I addressed the situation and received a pass/fail grade for the class. Over the next three years, many Black students experienced similar issues and concerns. In my junior year, my advisor in the business department challenged me when he informed me that he did not understand why I chose to write my thesis on Booker T. Washington's *Economic Aspects on Financing Tuskegee Institute*. I prevailed in my explanation and wrote my thesis. But it yet was another example of a judgment made on assumptions about race and background. I graduated a year later with my degree in business and a minor in education.

After graduation, I returned home to the Chicago area. That summer, I worked in the district business office of the high school that I had attended, waiting for the fall term to start so that I could work full time as a teacher and coach. I truly wanted a career in education, both in the classroom and in sports. I always thought that teaching was a very honorable profession, no matter where you work. Also, at the time, I did not understand the significance of being a small business owner and, quite frankly, I did not want to be a janitor.

But as fate would have it, it takes one decision, one experience, in my case one letter, to change or confirm life's expected direction. Described as a fateful letter of recommendation, the Iowa college business department advisor who challenged me in my thinking revealed doubts about my abilities and wrote:

> "I am glad that Rufus Glasper has decided to teach in the inner-city schools of Chicago because I doubt if he would ever make it in this highly competitive business world."

Forty-seven years later, I repeat the mean-spirited comments of betrayal and the undermined behavior and know the determination that they fostered in me that exists to this day. It was a life lesson that I take to heart every day and use as fuel in my role as an educational administrator.

A 2014 "Frontdoors" article refers to me as "Book Smart and Street Smart." I believe that everyone can be a student of life and that employers can unlock lived experiences and that this knowledge can be shared and proven as an integral part of the human experience.

In the 1970s, few African Americans were on educational institutions' business side in non-Black educational institutions. I chose in the summer of 1974 to use the "non-recommendation" to fuel my passion for succeeding and not let it derail my love for teaching and leadership. It also convinced me that only I could limit my education. So, I pursued further studies and earned a master's and an advanced degree in school business administration and a Doctorate of Philosophy in higher education finance. I also earned certification as a CPA.

I worked in school and college business offices for 29 years, including serving as the Director of Financial Planning and Budget for the Chicago Public Schools and as Chief Financial Officer for the Maricopa Community Colleges. In 2016, I retired as Chancellor of the Maricopa system and now serve as President and CEO of the League for Innovation in the Community College.

My brothers and sister took other paths. One brother graduated from college and worked as an insurance adjuster. My sister is a dentist and owns her practice. The other four brothers did not obtain a degree, but we have often discussed the world of work, its challenges, and their lived experiences. They chose to take paths that linked their personal learning to their desired level of economic opportunity. I paraphrase from Peter Smith, "When one is confident enough to fill to your own weaknesses (perceived or real), your chances of succeeding go way up."

Over the years, I have also used poems to express my thoughts and provide me with a release to take the next step and keep moving toward my goal. I think these ones also reflect on the value of this book.

Stick It Out by Rufus Glasper

As I reach the next level –I re-affirm my nearest goal
As I search within my past, I trust my future will unfold

As I seek a new beginning. I unleash the trepid me
A constant redefining of what I am, who I am, and where I want to be

I envision a freedom flow –of smiles, joy, sadness, and peace
I imagine a life worth living, with comforts that never cease

Though reality I cannot ignore – the pains of daily strife.
I move forward with a vengeance to make the best of my only Life.

To find my destiny—my beginning must never be in doubt
To accomplish what is mine – I have no choice but to stick it out.

From Denial to Commitment by Rufus Glasper

We live day by day in a Crisis of Change
We refute yet support the Denial of Reality
We exalt at the idea of being different, a Diversity of Existence
We develop maze-ways to provide deceptions for our Quest
We take the risk and conquer the challenge. We now have control
We seek the recognition, the commitment we ignore
We know the mission, we see the vision, but we lack the purpose
We strive to be multi-competent. Without it, we have little chance
We evolve from the pyramid to the circle
We thrive to enhance our participation and involvement but fail to make a choice.
We fake it until we make it
We are but like All the rest

In resistance we listen

Some see personal learning as the second tier of learning, not worthy of formal consideration in the workplace or in society. But our nation's unemployment is rising, and we also know that many pre-pandemic jobs will not return. Momentum is building in government and community ecosystems to redesign how educational institutions prepare Americans to take responsibility for learning and work as well as for democracy's future. We need to respect and support everyone and the learning they do—socially, civically, and economically—to solve the festering problems facing democracy at home and in the broader world.

It's 2021 and, in some senses, as I look back, too little has changed in 47 years. But the assault on democracy, the urgent need to reskill and upskill millions of American workers, and the inequities of social justice further revealed by the pandemic have brought us to an inflection point. They require education and business leaders to reimagine the workforce for the future of work and the good of the country. Let's begin that journey by taking a leadership role in restoring the "Soul of America." Let's occupy and settle *"The New Frontier of Learning and Work"!*

Introduction

Millions of Americans are blocked from achieving their economic, social, and civic potential by an education system that fails to capture and recognize their knowledge, skills, and abilities. At the heart of this systemic obstruction of opportunity lies our failure to understand and value personal learning. Using the life stories of personal learners, *Stories from the Education Underground* will unmask this blight and describe solutions that illustrate education's new frontier and bring innate American talent into public view.

To get at the heart of this problem, we must debunk the myth that college learning is the only learning beyond high school that matters. It is not. There are several paths to learning and career success in addition to the traditional college route. And your personal learning, the learning you do outside of college, matters just as much as college learning in many cases.

So, just what *is* personal learning? Personal learning is all that other learning that you do, learning that is not planned by schools and colleges. It includes learning:

- From your culture and personal traditions
- On the job, at home, and in the community
- With colleagues, supervisors, family, neighbors, and friends
- Directly from life experiences, as well as
- Via the computer, the library, or other data and information sources.

This may surprise you, but more than 80% of what we know comes from learning done outside of school. Personal learning is the driver and source of the vast majority of what we know and are able to do. This book celebrates the power of personal learning, arguing that it must be recognized as legitimate, useful knowledge not only by colleges but also in the workplace. Why? As a matter of simple justice, it is time to bring this massive natural and human resource from the margins to the mainstream of opportunity, education, and work in America.

If you don't have a college degree, all that learning, the talent that drives it, and the resulting knowledge and capacity gained are usually ignored, and economic opportunity denied. Why?

- Precisely because it isn't formal and because it has not traditionally qualified for academic credit or an employer credential, personal learning is usually unrewarded at colleges and workplaces.
- As a result, it goes unrespected by the larger society, which fails to see it as an important resource and contributor to a more fair and just social and economic narrative. Again, the equity and opportunity issues here are crystal clear.

"So, what's the big deal?" You may be thinking, "That's why we have colleges, isn't it?" Well, think of it this way. We all know the phrase, "That's just the tip of the iceberg." It refers to the fact that seven-eighths of an iceberg is underwater and out of sight. But it is still there, supporting the tip that we can see. If you are a ship's captain, you ignore it at your own peril. Remember the Titanic.

The same is true for your personal learning. The amount and shape of your knowledge are just like that iceberg. The "tip" is composed of knowledge that has been recognized and defined, usually by college degrees and certificates. The vast majority of your learning, however, is made up of the total package of your cultural background, aspirations, and lessons learned from mentors, as well as the knowledge, skills, and abilities you have gleaned from the experience of living. This personal learning lies below the surface of your life, unrecognized and largely invisible to you, your employers, and others.

This knowledge is extremely powerful and valuable. Your talent, self-learned skills, and capacity coupled with your background and lived experience, make you who you are. They comprise the lens through which you see and experience the world, including your employment and income. And they contribute to your aspirations for the future. But when colleges and employers ignore and devalue this powerful personal asset, they are not only hurting you; they are weakening society as well.

The American higher education ladder to opportunity, which has been assembled since World War II, leads to improved job opportunities and a better life for millions. It is a miracle of American democracy, and there is much to be proud of. But there is another side to the story. That same ladder to opportunity for some is also inaccessible to many others. And that lack of access contributes to the widening social and economic disparities and inequalities in our society.

Millions of people simply cannot adapt to the traditional collegiate model and its assumptions—financially, culturally, emotionally, or physically. In most cases, this is not a function of intelligence or native talent. Life circumstances simply get in the way. Some people have a high school diploma, and others have some college, but no certificate or degree. As a result, the only option to employ their talent and acquire knowledge is through personal and experiential learning, including non-collegiate training as they live and work.

But when there is no credit given for that learning, it generally does not lead to greater opportunities. Like the kids looking through the window at the candy store, these people are on the outside looking in, so close yet so far from realizing the opportunity they deserve.

Another harsh reality is that college, as it has been structured, has developed a paralyzing grip on our aspirations. On the one hand, it controls our sense of self-identity, self-esteem, and personal focus, as well as our sense of purpose in life. On the other hand, it also structures and controls our understanding of knowledge, competence, and economic and societal status. Furthermore, our current education and employment processes were not designed and organized to recognize the knowledge, skills, and abilities people have gained through personal learning. As a result, they are not converted into personal, academic, and economic value. Educators and employers too often pay attention only to the tip of the learning iceberg—credentials and degrees based on pre-determined curricular priorities at colleges—and ignore the rest. That's why I have previously referred to the knowledge, skills, and abilities gained through personal learning as "hidden credentials."

The sad fact is that, by separating college learning from personal learning, we weaken both. And as a result, higher education has become, however unintentionally, a significant contributor to the American income and equality gap that has grown so dramatically since the 1960s. It segregates the talent and the personal learning that does not include college as second-class and less important. And it promotes the economic payoff and resulting status of formally gained knowledge as the primary values which college provides. Given this bias, it is the height of irony that employers say that too many recent college graduates are not ready for work in their fields. Or, as one of the people I interviewed said, "While higher education may give you structure, build discipline and hold a whole slew of other benefits, the school of life can very well teach you everything you need to know to be successful."

On a personal level, imagine living in an environment where your essential being, your lived experience, your knowledge, your talent, and your traditions are treated as less important, second class. Such an environment would require that you construct your own sense of self-worth and self-esteem. This would leave you to make your way through high school and find your first job, all without a network of broader societal support and encouragement. Yet, that is exactly the task that we expect of more than 30 million adults, our fellow citizens, their friends, and families. And when we do that, we marginalize them, and we shortchange our society by compromising the value they have to contribute.

As Steve Lohr wrote in the *New York Times*, "As many as 30 million American workers without four-year college degrees have the skills to realistically move into new jobs that pay on average 70 percent more than their current ones......But the research also shows the challenges that workers face: They currently experience less income mobility than those holding a college degree, which is routinely regarded as a measure of skills. That widely shared assumption…is deeply flawed" (Dec. 3, 2020).

The good news is that America is beginning to think very differently about issues of fairness involving education, race, economic opportunity, and systemic discrimination. In fact, as Lohr further reported, "…hiring should be based on skills rather than degrees, as a matter of fairness and economic efficiency" (Dec. 3, 2020). That rethinking is leading to a new appreciation and respect for all the learning we do, including learning from culture, faith, life experience, college, and work. As respect for the value and power of personal learning grows, we are expanding our traditional beliefs to acknowledge that success through the traditional college experience is not the only way to identify knowledge and talent.

Stories from the Educational Underground will share the stories of previously marginalized people and the influence of life experience on their knowledge, well-being, and perspectives. The experiences described in these stories will show definitively that almost everyone has the innate capacity to learn and that they do so continually. Having said that, we have to remember that these are stories in which people, previously excluded because of their economic standing, race, indigenous origins, lack of post-secondary education, and/or other reasons, had to fight their way through to opportunity. The stories show how they struggled mightily to get their talent and capacity recognized. And they show the value of personal networks that ultimately connect them with opportunity, mentors who advise, challenge, and caution them at critical moments, and collegiate as well as non-collegiate programs that meet their needs in real time. These are all supports, which expedite the journey to opportunity and which college graduates generally enjoy.

These stories underscore the need for a new, more inclusive ecosystem for lifelong learning and work; an ecosystem that includes networks, mentoring, and timely programs and information. See *Harnessing America's Wasted Talent* (Smith, 2010) and *Long Life Learning* (Weise, 2021) for greater discussion of these issues. As a society, and as educators and employers, we need to respect, recognize, and harness life experience and the knowledge it generates, translating it into opportunity as smoothly and effectively as colleges have done for traditional learners over the years.

This new ecosystem will include college as we know it. But it will also include many other qualified options as well:

- non-traditional and alternative colleges
- new non-collegiate pathways for learning and work which carry formal recognition
- informal access to learning resources and
- the recognition of personal learning from life experience itself.

In the future, people will be able to move from one mode of learning to another, based on their needs and life situation, without penalty. Personal learning and flexible pathways are two keys to a more equitable and just future for all.

Two recent books have raised serious questions about the way colleges work, our use of norms to define quality, and the very notion of merit. In *The Merit Myth: How Our Colleges Favor the Rich and Divide America* (Carnevale et al., 2020), describe in detail how college degrees are, in and of themselves, discriminatory. The authors' larger point is that college heavily favors the more well-to-do members of our society. It brands them with an implied worth that, while valuable to them, is incomplete and not always entirely accurate. For millions of other people, the downside to this picture is exclusion and systemic discrimination based on race and income.

Todd Rose attacks the issue from another angle in *The End of Average: Unlocking Our Potential by Embracing What Makes Us Different* (2016). He argues that our penchant for averages and norms has homogenized expectations and measurements of success. This inherent value system has resulted in serious socio-cultural and economic consequences. Put another way, this homogenization is the enemy of individuality and the differences among people. As a result, it hides the uniqueness and value that individuals and cultures embody, and that personal learning represents.

Each book questions, in its own way, our definition and understanding of what constitutes valuable knowledge and how to attain it. They also question the definition of educational quality, including the unquestioned value of college as it currently operates. And the "sameness" which that homogeneity creates, including its treatment of most personal learning, is inherently exclusionary.

Ask yourself these questions.

- Are the norms of a "dominant culture," for example, America's white culture, the only valuable norms?
- Are people who graduate from college more worthy or better than people who do not?
- Is there only one way to "do" college in terms of organization, content, cost, structure, timing, values, and goals?
- Are there other ways to recognize talent, capacity, and knowledge?
- Is diversity within and across our society a source of strength to be developed or a weakness to be treated and reduced?

America's learning and work landscape must incorporate personal learning and the talent and capacity that drives it as an explicit and inherently valuable component of a person's knowledge. This expanded definition of knowledge is far more inclusive than simply knowing a great deal about a particular subject, be it accounting, computer technology, nuclear physics, or Hegelian philosophy. It includes two additional dimensions.

The first is comprised of cross-cutting intellectual capacities such as problem-solving, critical thinking, and analytical skills. They describe *what* you are able to do with the knowledge you have acquired. The second includes emotional intelligences and how they contribute to critical abilities such as communication, effective teamwork, promoting diversity, and leadership. Emotional intelligence determines *how* you will employ the knowledge you have gained. When understood through the lens of all three dimensions, this enhanced definition of knowledge will provide a warm home for millions of people whose talent and capacity have previously been excluded.

Stories from the Educational Underground will focus on personal learning as a common denominator among people. As they reflect on these stories, readers will sense the power of their own personal learning and better understand its value. Importantly, they will also be exposed to the personal, societal, and economic costs that accrue when personal learning is marginalized and ignored.

Recognizing and respecting personal learning, those hidden credentials, for college and employment value have slowly increased. And when college and life experience learning come together, the whole is greater than the sum of its parts.

A few years ago, I spoke with a man who had returned to college later in life and had assessed his personal learning for credit. He told me:

> I was totally divorced from any knowledge of my personal learning. Had no idea what was in there. But as I got going, I saw my life rolling out in front of me. It was incredible……I was astonished at how much I had forgotten about what I had done and what it had meant to me… I loved the experience, and it changed my life…When I first dove into it, I was afraid there was no 'there, there.' Boy, was I wrong.

There are two elements to this story. First, since he couldn't adapt to college as a young man, he thought he had surrendered the opportunity that college offered. Second, as a consequence, he didn't think he knew anything much. Although the first concern was largely true at the time, the second was totally wrong. And the boost to his self-esteem when he got that validation literally leaps off the page at you.

We are leaving millions of people and a great deal of talent and capacity on the far side of a massive opportunity gap that hurts individuals. When such learning has not been captured as part of your educational or employment records or recognized as having societal value, your knowledge and your credentials often remain hidden, and your future is compromised.

But, as bad as it is for individuals, the gap is also bad for society. Contrary to the myth of America as the land of opportunity, if you are born poor, are a person of color, or a member of an indigenous community, too often, your chances for educational success, economic opportunity, and security are far more limited than if you are not. So, closing this gap is also a critical social justice issue. When it is analyzed along economic and racial lines, the systemic disparities and the gross inequalities are crystal clear, and the divisions created by privilege appear. Put more bluntly, if we are going to end systemic discrimination in education, work, and the larger society, we must encourage, respect, and reward talent and knowledge in all of its forms and regardless of how it was gained. And recognizing the importance and the power of personal learning lies at the heart of this conversation.

It is time we closed the gap, recognizing and celebrating a diverse American societal and cultural DNA, which includes cultural background, life experience, knowledge, and learning. There is plenty of data to chronicle the gap and make this case. But data is not flesh and blood. It is time we heard from America's previously excluded personal learners—good people, hard-working people, smart people—as they describe their struggles to achieve opportunity and get value for their hidden credentials. They will describe their lives, their work, and the creation of their knowledge and talent. And they will share the benefits they have accumulated, along with the losses they suffered and the opportunities they were denied along the way.

I will share the life stories of people who started life on the far side of that opportunity gap. But we must remember that they are success stories, the exception to the rule. They have overcome the obstacles to opportunity through persistence, patience, and hard work. And, in a few cases, they simply bypassed those obstacles like a hurdler going over a hurdle. All in all, they are heroes and survivors of a process that was stacked against them.

Bringing the power of their learning and its value in their lives—their hidden credentials—into broad daylight will point the way to a happier, fairer, and more economically just society. And seeing how to realize the personal as well as academic and economic value for hidden credentials will put power where it belongs, in the hands of every person.

Consider the impact of the COVID-19 pandemic. We experienced vividly the vulnerability of workers trapped by work circumstances which were often determined by life circumstances, systemic discrimination, and/or a lack of formal education. They were trapped between a rock (economic necessity) and a hard place (the pandemic). I want to break that trap, shining a bright light on personal learning through life experience as a powerful source of talent. Talent, when recognized and respected, can create greater economic opportunity, greater economic security, increased self-esteem, and a more just and healthy society.

Stories From the Education Underground: The New Frontier for Learning and Work has three purposes. The first is for each of us to recognize, value, and reflect on the personal learning we do and its impact on us. Understanding your personal learning gives you more control over your life, no matter who you are. The second is to illustrate the human and societal costs of the way we currently treat many learners and to argue for a new way of thinking about them. And the third is to describe programs and pathways which will create the new ecosystem we need and provide the needed support to personal learners throughout life.

As I have experienced these things professionally, thought about them, and discussed them with others, I have come to the following understandings.

- The traditional college experience usually confirms mainstream cultural and intellectual expectations. And success in college often includes acceptance of those expectations, consciously or unconsciously.
- Life experience—our culture and background as well as lived experience—is our one "true" teacher, bringing the deepest learning we do and forming the foundation of our understanding of the world. As important as it is, however, this learning lies beyond traditional definitions of education and is often de-valued.
- When life experience learning is marginalized, it devalues talent and can deepen existing divisions of culture, race, and economics.

- When life experience is respected, recognized, and augmented with focused learning, whether college or other, the whole is greater than the sum of its parts, and more diverse populations are recognized.
- Currently, there is a lot of talent and capacity that regularly goes unrecognized and, therefore, untapped.

We all bring cultural perspectives, talent, knowledge, skills, and abilities gained outside of traditional higher education to the table. Consider the following nuggets of American folklore.

> Live and Learn.
> The School of Hard Knocks.
> Older, But Wiser.

We have all heard these sayings. They affirm an understanding that life has important lessons and that you will become more knowledgeable and accomplished as the years pass. In each saying, the message is similar. You can learn from the experience of living. There are strong and useful connections between effort, learning, and success. If you are resourceful, work hard, and learn on your feet, opportunity will come knocking. This folklore is part of the American promise: Everyone will have a seat at the table of opportunity if they work hard and play by the rules. And it suggests that all will be treated with equal respect.

Unfortunately, our folklore is far from the reality that many Americans endure. These stories from the "learning underground" will describe what it is like to struggle and fight simply to have a chance for that promise of increased opportunity, recognition, respect, and reward. And, in reporting the successes that some truly heroic people have had in overcoming or bypassing these obstacles, it will advocate for making the recognition of personal learning part of the pathway to opportunity and success in the new ecosystem of learning and work. These learners must bring their unique talents from the margin to society's mainstream and get credit where credit is due.

Here's what you will find in this book. We think of life as a linear journey. In fact, however, for many people, life is dominated by uncontrolled happenstance, which is framed by a lack of resources. That lack leads to a revolving door of jobs gained and lost, unsuccessful attempts at college, and personal circumstances that have made a linear journey impossible. For others, people with ADHD, other disabilities, or those who needed "hands-on" learning, the way schools are organized was an obstacle to success. And running throughout these stories is the consistent sub-text of discrimination by race and economic status. While the people in this book ultimately succeeded, they were fighting a status quo stacked against them the whole way.

While each of the life stories that follow are unique, they generally share common defining elements, including hard and uncertain circumstances early in life dictated by income, race, and other insecurities. In case after case, the lives into which these people were born dictated the realities they faced during their early years. In virtually every case, they needed to fight to change the arc of their life to even have a chance at succeeding.

Two other common elements among the stories are turning points and transitions. Turning points are those moments when you realize you have come to a crossroads in your life and things need to change. They are triggering events that propel you on a new course. And life transitions are what come next; when learners change course and seek a new future. In most cases, transitions drive further learning and greater understanding.

The stories will also include the reflections of personal learners as they think back on their learning journey and transitions and understand how their perspectives on life have changed over time. What did those events mean to them? How did the recognition of their knowledge affect them? And how did their personal understanding of their life journey deepen and evolve at various stages of their lives?

Look for all these elements in each of the life stories which follow:

- the beginning of life's journey
- the impact of work and life experience on learning
- turning points and transitions and
- reflection on the larger meaning they extract from their lived experience and personal learning.

I have organized the interviews into four sections. In Section One, I share "My Story" as a stark contrast to the ensuing core narratives and the lives described in *Stories from the Educational Underground*. "My Story" describes how I benefitted tremendously from white privilege from day one. For me, college and life thereafter have been a reaffirmation and extension of life as I understood and anticipated it. "My Story" will illustrate the power of having your cultural background, life experience, and education intertwine in an accepted societal DNA, something we should want for everyone.

Section Two describes three types of "Learning Journeys" focusing on critical characteristics of the learners' journeys, including the life circumstances they faced.

- People on "The Merry-Go-Round" were constantly caught in an up-and-down, in and out experience with work, life, and college that left them dizzy and confused for years as they tried to sort things out. These folks are the epitome of people who were losing a fight that they never chose because that choice was determined at birth. But still, they found a way to jump off the merry-go-round and seize their future.
- The "Dreams Deferred: One Step at a Time" folks are just that. They are as determined and resolute as they are frustrated. But they let life unfold and seized opportunities when they arose, finally getting to a better future for themselves and their families.
- The stories in "On Their Own Terms: Self-Directed Learners" capture the power and extent of personal learning in life. These people got bumped around and, in some cases slammed, by life. But they drew on their native intelligence and personal learning and found the path that worked for them, going over, under, around, and when necessary, through the obstacles before them.

Section Three, "Bridges to the Future," focuses on the people, programs, and colleges that, collectively, formed the opportunity networks which these "underground learners" finally accessed.

- "Important People and Programs" describes how learners benefitted tremendously from people they met along the way; people who advised and advocated for them. Much is made of mentoring and support. But for advice to be truly helpful, it should be connected to a pathway towards opportunity. And the impact of these "important people" in learners' lives and the programs to which they connected the learners cannot be overestimated.
- Then "Colleges That Helped" shares stories about some of the different and innovative college models and the services they offered, which made them a true "bridge to the future" for the learners involved.

Finally, Section Four, "Michael's Story—The Capstone," shares one powerful story that touches all the bases described up to that point. "Michael's Story" powerfully illustrates the two main points of *Stories from the Educational Underground*—the presence of enormous innate talent and intelligence just waiting to be recognized and encouraged and the power of personal learning. Michael shares his life journey and learning to date.

His story illustrates how gaining opportunity in life can be a journey that often contradicts powerful parts of your cultural background, history, and daily reality. And yet, drawing on his personal learning as well as formal education and great advice and support along the way, Michael persisted through thick and thin to a remarkable place of insight, knowledge, and understanding after 36 years.

As you will undoubtedly notice, most of the people interviewed have, like Michael, learning journeys, bridges to the future, and experiences that could fit in all of the subgroups in sections two and three. Peoples' life journeys are not one-dimensional. They are truly multifaceted. But I have tried to align the dominant characteristics of each story with the section in question to highlight more clearly the different realities experienced by most personal learners who couldn't access traditional approach to college.

The Conclusion addresses the basic assertions of this narrative. It rolls them up into a call to understand that, in addition to being an education issue, linking personal learning and economic opportunity is a social justice issue as well.

Finally, the Appendix will include information about "New Pathways for Learning and Work," including many of the organizations covered in the book as examples. I will describe emerging alternatives which, taken collectively, suggest what the dominant characteristics of a new ecosystem could well be when it is fully organized. This is not a comprehensive list by any means. These programs and services are, however, good examples of current practices in this emerging ecosystem.

Section 1: My Story

My personal learning has taught me a lot about my great privilege, which is, to this day, supported by and embedded in systemic discrimination and white privilege.

This book is filled with life stories that are very different than mine. These people were not born to privilege. They have lived on the other side of the opportunity gap and made the transition. They have all done well, while some have excelled. Millions of others just like them, however, have been frustrated and limited by the life circumstances they were born into.

So, before I interviewed other people about their life stories, I thought I ought to interview myself and briefly tell my story. In contrast to their life journeys, privilege launched mine and has protected me throughout my life in situations where others would probably have been left by the roadside. We are all personal learners. But my personal learning was aided and abetted, indeed infused, by privilege and college. If the practice of justice rides on the shoulders of respect, then I have received both. But this should be the case for millions of others as well.

Privilege and its first cousin, a society in which opportunity is segregated by income and race, may be contrasted with the lives of "others"—low-income people, people of color, women, and the LGBTQ community. These "others," including white men and women shackled by poverty and lack of education, are often referred to as "underprivileged." In reality, they have been denied the fundamental characteristics of privilege: being given the benefit of the doubt, having their life experience respected by the larger society, and gaining access to opportunity through networks of friends and associates.

It is hard for some people who have benefitted from white privilege to accept the fact that they have benefitted from something that, in their minds, doesn't explain them personally. But here is the thing: white privilege, "the way things are," is not personal. It is systemic, woven into the fabric of our society. And, while a rising tide lifts all boats, white privilege only lifts some of them.

Privilege is mainly about white men, those of us who benefit from its gifts. Let me be clear, privileged people are not bad people, per se. Many of us are kind and well-intentioned. Some work to improve the lives of others; some are caring and raise their children to be so as well, while still others strive to be decent employers and community builders. And, yes, some are selfish and self-interested, looking for ways to bolster and fortify the privilege they were born with while working to actively deny others the same thing. But none of that is the point. Taken collectively, the impact of privilege, as things are currently structured, constitutes a control of opportunity for the majority who are born outside its warm embrace.

Frankly, I put myself in the former category of privileged men. I have worked throughout my life to improve the lives of others with the best of intentions and to raise a beautiful, caring, and committed family. I am married to a woman whose life story is, in and of itself, remarkable. But wherever I fit on that human scale, however I have behaved, and whatever my intentions might have been, I was born into a vastly preferred situation, one where the road ahead was paved and included comfort stops, off-ramps, and bridges to get me over and around the hard times. Most other people experience life as a crapshoot of income, health, housing security, educational opportunity, and respect, or a lack thereof.

Let me be clear. I am not writing out of a sense of guilt about the privilege I was born with. I was damn lucky. I have tried to use my advantages for social change and a leveling of the playing field throughout my life, creating innovative higher education models that serve previously under-served adults. I bypassed the "big money" for service, often on what were considered the margins of accepted practice at the time. But it was my choice to follow the path that I did. And being able to have and control your choices in life is, in and of itself, an extraordinary expression of privilege.

I am writing because, after more than 50 years as an adult in my privileged American world, I believe the control and definition of opportunity by the privileged will ultimately destroy us if we do not understand and act on its destructive consequences. I am from Vermont, and snow stories are part of my background. So here is my metaphor about the ultimate impact of privilege of democracy.

In Vermont, one of the things you learn about winter is that the salt used to de-ice the roads can accumulate on your car's undercarriage, slowly rusting the metal away. You don't see it or feel it until your bumper falls off!

Privilege is a little bit like that salt, corroding the structure of democracy in largely unseen ways. It benefits the few while structurally denying many people opportunity, respect, and security, all the while implicitly blaming them for the failure that has been cast upon them. I don't want America's bumpers to fall off.

This opportunity chasm is not simply "their" problem, whoever they are. Yes, it happens to them. But it is "our" problem as a society. We all pay for it—humanly, ethically, morally, and financially—on a daily basis. And ultimately, I fear that our societal bumpers will fall off. So, I am hoping that the power of the stories of those who have been marginalized will be better understood when seen through the lens of one who was not.

◆ ◆ ◆

I was raised in a marvelous extended family, most of whose forebears migrated to Vermont or the greater northeast from the British Isles in the late 1700s and early 1800s. In their land of opportunity, they quickly became doctors and lawyers, teachers and poets, and musicians, scientists, and bankers.

To further illustrate our historically embedded privilege, consider this. Several of my great aunts and one of my grandmothers graduated from college, one with a master's degree in Social Work, before 1920! And, to my knowledge, my grandfathers, their brothers, my father, my mother, and all of my uncles and aunts were part of the 4% of Americans who had a college degree by the early 1940s. My family had an iron-clad grip on the future that I was born into.

Unsurprisingly, that tradition continued into my generation. Along with a little quirkiness, which ran throughout all the generations, we became bankers, entrepreneurs, doctors, educators and non-profit executives, and musicians, poets, and artists, among other things. We were raised to "give back," to believe that taxes are the responsibility of those with means, to wish the best for everyone, and to level the playing field for all - civically, socially, and economically.

And yet, looking back on it all, we were in an impenetrable bubble of privilege, one which protected us unless we chose to purposefully break out of it. And, to my recollection, other than my two uncles who were killed in WWII, none of us did.

The extended Smith, Pease, Hewitt, Finlay clan privilege was established on our skin color, a foundation of leadership in the community over decades, the respect of others, plenty of money (by any reasonable standard), great housing, strong higher education credentials, good health, and high expectations. And as I grew up in the late 1940s and 1950s, it never occurred to me that all these elements were anything other than the way life was. As I look back on it, however, I can see that they were a significant departure from the status quo that surrounded me.

If there is one word that describes my first 15 years of life, it would be "secure." Along with the usual ups and downs, my main worries were Little League baseball, girls, my newspaper route, the Boy Scouts, and doing well in school. As the saying goes, "life was good."

The first time I needed a bridge over problems that might have derailed another kid came in the ninth grade. I was president of the student council at Burlington Junior High School and having a great time. Except for Algebra. I had been slowly slipping in math beginning in the eighth grade. And, as I neared the mid-year, I was in the soup. Despite everyone's best efforts, including mine, I was failing.

For others, unless they changed course and somehow survived Algebra, this could well have been a cause for lowered expectations, possibly repeating a year, and/or, ultimately, a downward shift in aspirations. Not so for me.

I applied to Phillips Academy Andover (or rather my father applied for me), was accepted, and repeated ninth grade there in 1960. Ten years later, I had completed Andover, Princeton University with high honors in History (where I figured out how to avoid math and science), the Harvard Graduate School of Education, and started a college that operates to this day. For me, when a significant problem arose, there was an off-ramp that got me around an otherwise significant obstacle.

What a ride it was! Yes, I learned a lot inside but, as I later realized, probably more outside of the classroom during those ten years. For example, at Princeton one day, my professor threw me out of his preceptorial (a small class where you must be prepared) because I was not prepared and was acting out. He told me to wait outside. At the end of the class, he came out, put me up against the wall, and said, "Don't you ever waste my time again! You are smart. And there is much to be done in the world. Act that way!" Dr. David Flaherty changed my life that day. But it wasn't a history lesson he taught me. It was a life experience and life purpose lesson.

I also had a string of interesting summer jobs—working as a boat hand on a ferry boat where I polished brass, cleaned toilets, and learned about the importance of showing up on time; digging ditches for a construction company, and working in a lawn mowing business. As my father hoped at the time, these jobs would stimulate me to go to college and develop a professional career.

I attended the Colorado Outward Bound School when I was 18 and then, two years later, The National Outdoor Leadership School (NOLS). I was always able to take four weeks off from work to do these things. And it didn't occur to me that this flexibility alone was a function of privilege, that I could afford to take the time off. Having said that, I loved the learning that I did at these places. And, although I could not see it at the time, these experiences stimulated the initial formation of my professional life and love affair with experiential and personal learning.

In retrospect, this Vermont guy who thought he knew a lot about the woods figured that Outward Bound would be a snap. Interesting and exciting, but an extension of what he already knew. But once there, he learned about the team; that the kid who could read the map accurately and the kid who could get a fire going in the rain were key members of the team. It wasn't all about walking in the woods, being strong and energetic. And I had to keep a journal every night. It sounds innocuous, but as a result, I internalized details, including the names of the guys I tented with and some lessons of leadership that I would never have remembered otherwise.

At the National Outdoor Leadership School, I encountered tragedy and a set of circumstances that led me away from extreme outdoor activity and towards experiential learning as an educational strategy. A member of my patrol fell while rock climbing and died. Three of us sat with him, mortally wounded and barely breathing, stretched across our legs for several hours until a rescue could be executed from the middle of the rock face on which we had been climbing. When he was inverted to be lowered down the cliff, he died.

That was bad enough. But it elicited an Ayn Randian response from some of the counselors, "That's part of the game, the risk you take, when you climb. It's you and the rock face." Maybe so for them and some others. But for me, the outdoors and experiential learning were not life or death existential matters. They were ways to experience life and, as I have indicated earlier, learn about yourself and others. And so, my attention turned to using and reflecting on experience and the learning it generates as tools to generate learning.

There was a lot of learning in all of these episodes. But, and this is the most important thing for me to share as I look back on it all, none of it would have happened if my father had not been able to "fix" the problem back in ninth grade by sending me to Andover. When Robert Frost wrote, "Two roads diverged in a yellow wood and I took the one less traveled by," I believe he was talking about risk, venturing out on your own. In my case, however, the road less traveled was the preferred road of protection and privilege, where any danger was anticipated, a road which was not available to most others.

Another critical case in point. In 1967 and 68, with the Vietnam War raging, I, along with thousands of others, wrestled with the question of whether to serve in the armed services. As a Summer Intern in Congressman Robert Stafford's (R-Vt.) office, I had had a taste of the politics up close and personal. And I did not like the war. My mother had freed me emotionally with her advice and support, "To thine own heart be true."

Ultimately, however, I decided that I was not a conscientious objector and applied to Officer Candidate School. To my horror, I was turned down because I have birth defects, malformed hip and shoulder sockets, which were (and still are) incomplete and can be easily dislocated. And equally as bad, I had also been turned down at all the graduate schools I applied to because I was 1A. Talk about a Catch-22!

So, just two weeks after graduating from Princeton, with X-rays of my hips and shoulders and a doctor's letter in hand, I went to my draft physical in Albany, NY. At the end of the day, the x-rays provided the evidence that excluded me from the draft. I confess that I was very relieved. And riding home on the bus, I made a commitment to myself to live a life that mattered as a result of the gift I had been given.

The deeper point, however, is this. Without the confidence and support of my family and the income to get the x-rays and associated doctor's opinion, I would have been drafted and probably have landed in Vietnam, with or without malformed sockets. And, for the second time, without this "off-ramp" around an obstacle on the highway of life supported by privilege, what followed would have been very different.

But the future, as they say, lay ahead. The next day, with my deferral in hand, I called my mentor at Princeton. He then called Harvard, where I had previously been turned down because I was 1A, and I was off to graduate school on two weeks' notice! All this happened within one month of my graduation from college. Not bad.

The biggest decisions I made along that road in the next two years were to become an educator and, ultimately, to return to Vermont. Basically, other than the draft thing, most of my life was just rolling by, and it was, generally, pretty damn good.

Becoming an educator involved breaking from my father's hope that I would follow in his steps as a lawyer and mutual savings banker. I loved my dad. And, while I was proud of the fact that our family history lay in mutual savings banking, the non-profit side of banking, I simply did not want that path. And so, with a loan in my pocket (from another bank) and my father's admonition, "Goodbye Mr. Chips"—in other words, "Don't 'just' be a teacher" —ringing in my ears, I set off for Cambridge in the summer of 1968, just two weeks after my deferral (Hilton, 1934).

But what kind of an educator would I be? To my astonishment, my student teaching experience taught me what I wouldn't be doing. I didn't like teaching in a classroom. I had a negative gut reaction to the experience. I didn't like how I behaved. I didn't like how I felt. And I didn't like the relationship that high school required between teachers and students.

One story captures the essence of my discomfort. I was teaching at Charlestown High School, in a working-class community outside of Boston. There was a young man in my senior history class, we'll call him Steve. Steve had been generally very active in class, spoke up, participated, and generally did well. Then as the spring term progressed, he became increasingly quiet, dozed off from time to time, was incomplete on his homework, and failing his tests. He was on the way to failing.

After class one day, I asked Steve what was going on? Why was his performance nose-diving? And he replied, with a sparkle in his eye, "Oh, Mr. Smith, I know it hasn't been good. But the good news is that I have been accepted at Wentworth Tech! I'll be the first in my family to go to college. And I had to get a second job to cover the tuition. So, I have been pretty tired. I'm sorry, I'll try to pick it up a little."

And I was going to fail him, screwing his chances of going to college! If I hadn't asked him, that is what would have happened. But knowing the situation, frankly, I gave him a C+, he graduated, and the rest is history. My student teaching, as I later came to understand, taught me that I needed to work in educational settings and ultimately create educational settings other than the traditional classroom.

There are many other stories, but the other critical story concerns my decision to return to Vermont after I graduated from Harvard. I had been thinking about going to Alaska, where my sister Susan lived, and becoming an outdoor educator. After my experience with Steve, I thought the outdoors was the classroom for me. With my experience at the Outward Bound and the National Outdoor Leadership Schools and with my teaching degree in hand, that seemed like a sensible and slightly adventurous path. But something was nagging at me.

One day I realized that the Alaskan path, as interesting and adventurous as it seemed, was also fueled by a fear that my family, its reputation and reach, would dominate me if I went back home. Then, with a searing insight, I realized that, if that were my fear, it would dominate me wherever I went; that the problem was mine, not theirs. I said to myself, "Face it, Peter. You could be in Spain, penniless because you were robbed. And if you could beg a dime (It *was* 1969) and call home, you would be ok." It was a critically important personal reckoning. But it did not change the fact of my privilege, just how I was going to handle it.

So, I bit the bullet, went back to Vermont, got married, rented an apartment in Montpelier, and started a family. My earlier insight allowed me to structure my career in Vermont as I wished, pursuing career pathways in education that featured experiential learning and were on the margins of accepted practice at that time. But I was where I wanted to be, doing what I wanted to do. And I had made the choices. I was pulled by my dreams, not pushed by necessity or any other life force.

First, I worked for the Commissioner of Education. Harvey Scribner was an up-from-the-bottom man from rural Maine. He was the first in his family to go to college. And he was a fighter for previously disenfranchised learners. Under his guidance, I designed and implemented a for-credit service-learning program for high school juniors called Do Unto Others (DUO). There was nothing else like it in the state. The excitement in high schools among the faculty and students was keen, and the stories about the impact of the kids' experiences were wonderful. As I remember it, we had 12-15 high schools employing the program by the end of the first year.

After I left the State Department of Education, I started a street academy for high school dropouts called the Montpelier Educational Facility. It was a second chance facility aimed at using community resources to stop the drop-out spiral. There was plenty of reading and writing, but the community, its institutions, problems, and assets, was our classroom.

Then in the fall of 1970, I became the Executive Director of a state commission that quickly evolved into the Community College of Vermont (CCV), now over 50 years old. And that's where my "formal" professional and public life of service began.

I am very proud of the work I did in the ten years between 1969 and 1978. And I believe that, as I have in later parts of my career, I brought some strong personal talent, energy, commitment, vision, and, increasingly, professional experience to it. But let's take a step back and understand some of the reasons beyond me, reasons of my privilege, that helped it all happen.

Throughout this period of time, I was constantly aware that what I was doing might fail—financially, educationally, and/or politically. The Community College of Vermont (CCV) was a radical experiment for its time. It was a community-based college, with no campus and no full-time faculty, operating more in the fashion of the field-based Agricultural Extension Service.

We offered credit for life experience as well as courses that led to degrees. Initially, we operated during the evenings and on the weekends, in high schools, vocational centers, living rooms, church basements, and Head Start centers. CCV was designed to adapt to the lives of working adults and to take higher education to the "end of the dirt road" for Vermonters who couldn't get it any other way. That was our core aspiration. And, as a result, it was very controversial among traditional educators as well as some others.

But we also had an invisible friend and protector: my privilege. Looking back on it, there were several aspects to this. First, though I worried about the college failing, I never doubted my right to be trying to establish it. I was meant to be there doing what I was doing. I had chosen to do it.

Beyond that, however, why was a Republican Governor willing to give us (me, the Smith kid) a chance? Why did the father of Vermont K-12 education, A. John Holden, agree to advise the effort pro bono? When I approached the Vermont State Colleges and negotiated the arrangement that ultimately made us a member of the system, did it matter that I had known the Provost all of my life and that every member of the Board of Trustees knew my family? And, when the college finally received its first appropriation, and my father was a member of the State Senate appropriations committee, did it matter that he left the room before the vote, saying, "You folks have to decide this without me. I have a minor conflict of interest"?

I think you get the point. Even when I was doing controversial things (in some people's eyes), I got the benefit of the doubt every step of the way precisely because of who I was and my family's history. If CCV was going to fail, it would be on the merits and the related politics. That's privilege.

This takes nothing away from the vision for the college, the extraordinary people working to make it happen, those who succeeded us, the learners who risked their hopes on us, and, collectively, all who made the college what it has become today. But I believe that, in our early years, we were given the air to breathe for five reasons: we had a great idea and an extraordinary team, we worked our butts off, the time and the timing were right, we had some lucky breaks, and we were, in subtle ways, shielded by my privilege. Ultimately, we were given the benefit of the doubt. CCV would be judged on its merits.

Happily, CCV redefined educational opportunity in Vermont. To be frank, however, the CCV effort and all that went before it defined my personal and professional life.

There have been other turning points in my life. As I look back, my political career, which ended when I lost my seat in the United States Congress because of my position on gun control (favoring banning AK-47s), was a brutal transition. I had listened in an informal Education and Labor meeting as a young woman from Anacostia High School described her fear of going to school because of guns. I had asked her what she thought she needed more of to succeed in high school. She replied, "Courage. Because then, when the gangbangers on the corner would threaten me with their guns on my way to school because I wanted to go to college, I could walk up to them, put my finger on their chin, and say, 'Get out of my way! I'm going to college! But I just slink on by and keep moving." And I thought to myself, "This isn't about 22 rifles and deer hunting in Vermont. This is about constant fear in her life. And she thinks that she needs more courage! I've got to do something." The next day I signed on to sponsor a bill banning AK-47s.

So, that was the turning point. I lost the next election. And though I regretted losing, I never regretted taking on the issue of guns. At that point, however, after running in seven elections over 12 years (for the State Senate, Lt. Governor, Governor, and Congress) and winning four, I reached a conclusion. I liked politics more than it liked me. If I went four for seven in a baseball career, I would be batting .570, a Hall of Fame average. But in politics, it was too low. It meant that the alignment just wasn't right.

So, I returned to education and have enjoyed an incredible 30 plus years since then. Once again, building on my background and what had been a strong career to date, things worked out. It is all of a piece. First, I needed a bridge to opportunity. Dr. Robert Atwell, the CEO of the American Council on Education (ACE), a leading national educational association, gave me a short-term contract to research and write an article. And then, I became the interim director of a national commission on financial aid supported by Senator Jim Jeffords. (I-Vt.)

That bought me the time to get into the marketplace and, among other things, meet Stephen Joel Trachtenberg, President of George Washington University. As a result, I became Dean of the Graduate School of Education and Human Services at the George Washington University. Then, after four years there, I was hired to be the founding President of California State University Monterey Bay. Frankly, I had opportunities galore. But the short-term contracts that Dr. Atwell and Senator Jeffords secured for me paved the way back to opportunity.

Then came the moment in 2000 when I was diagnosed with severe ADHD. At the time, I was in my fifth year as the founding president of California State University, Monterey Bay. And things were not going as well as I would have liked. I had always been "energetic" and impulsive as well as optimistic and hard-working. But there were times when I couldn't remember what had been said or decided; times when I jumped to conclusions and acted without sufficient self-control.

Being able to get some counseling, self-diagnose and then ultimately go to a doctor were huge benefits. After I took the diagnostic test called TOVA (Test of Variable Attributes) and began my medication, I came to understand that, for all its ups and downs, my experience of life up to that point was like looking at a black and white television with "snow." It was as if I was skimming the surface, not diving into the depths.

And that turning point, that new perspective, gave me the opportunity to finish my work at CSUMB successfully. By the time I resigned six years later, the college was positioned to become a leading institution in California and the Western region. And the faculty and ensuing administrations have converted a very promising start into a current-day success story.

Understanding that you are processing information differently than most people is a shock. What does it mean going forward? How do I adjust? But, once again, there was a comfort stop along the highway of life not available to others. At this comfort stop, I could get help because of my position, the advice I could get, my insurance, my medication, and my standing in the community. Never a mention of losing my job or other consequences, though those might have been on the table in the next couple of years without the treatment. And those benefits have continued to this day.

My life went from "black and white with snow" to "Hi-Def 3D color TV" overnight.

As I reflect on my experiences in California, and then subsequently at the United Nations Education, Science, and Culture Organization (UNESCO) in Paris, and working in online education, currently at the University of Maryland Global Campus, there were several lessons, decisions, and results that were consequences of earlier events in my life. My life lessons in the "School of Hard Knocks" informed my performance and my understanding of work and personal life as I went forward.

But, given my privilege, I never doubted that I was meant to be where I was, doing what I was doing. There are times when you simply have to stand and fight, regardless of the consequences. For me, those times included the Community College of Vermont, the gun control issue in Congress, founding Cal State Monterey Bay, and leading a significant reform at UNESCO's Education Sector.

Right or wrong, sometimes it comes down to conscience and conviction. Happily, I had both. But importantly, I could afford to have both, act on them, and survive to tell the story. And here's the thing. I didn't win all the fights. I won some and lost others. But I never lost a fight I didn't choose. And I always had the assistance needed to stand up and continue after I lost a fight.

As that reality dawned on me, I realized there were millions of people in this country and around the world who are losing fights every day that they never asked for. And when they lose, game over. That was that. My advantage, the ability to choose my fights and get support when needed, has deepened and informed my definition of privilege as well as my commitment to break down the barriers experienced by others.

Also, when faced with a difficult and controversial decision, personal or professional, I learned to ask, "Will the world (the environment I am living and working in) be a better place because of this decision?" If the answer is "yes," then proceed. But if the answer is "no," then you have to ask yourself, why are you pursuing it? Is it a personal preference that is not best for the organization or the situation?

Another way of understanding this came from something I heard from Col. Hank Hendrickson, retired Army officer and one of the great and stalwart pioneers at Cal State Monterey Bay. One day, we were discussing a difficult decision and Hank said, "You know, we used to say in the Army, if you want it bad, you're gonna get it bad." In that case, I wanted it bad, and I changed my mind after his advice.

And, after years of leading teams comprised of people who knew more than I did, I realized that if you are confident enough to "fill to your weaknesses" when hiring and promoting, your chances of succeeding as a leader and a team go way up. This understanding grew originally from my experience in a singing group at Princeton, the Tigertones. I was easily one of the three weakest voices in the group. No solos for me, though I could harmonize and blend well enough. However, when the time came, I made a good president of the group. Being excellent at one thing, like solo singing, does not mean that you will be excellent in a related function, like being president of the group. And vice versa.

So, as you go through life, you "live and learn." I call it personal learning, which creates and deepens what I have come to call your hidden credentials. We all have them. And as I have, we all encounter turning points that determine direction and have consequences, positive and negative, for the future. Finally, there is the ability to learn how to reflect and draw meaning from the circumstances and the situations of your life as you grow older. These are all common features of our lives, whoever we are and wherever we come from. They are great sources of power and talent.

Each of these learning and life experiences informed and changed my life in incremental ways. And collectively, they have helped me understand my privilege and its preferential advantage as I have lived along the way.

Getting the value from life that my privilege and my life experiences have given me is far from common and not as readily available to many people. Everybody learns throughout life. Far fewer people get rewarded for and reinforced by that learning and are able to use it to create a better life for them and their family. It took the trifecta from hell—the COVID-19 pandemic, the killings of George Floyd and others, and the economic and social disruption of the lives of essential workers, people of color, and older and poorer Americans—to permanently clarify the depth and persistence of that harsh reality for me. As I said earlier, I am proud of much of what I have accomplished in life. But I have never lost a fight I didn't choose, while millions of other Americans are losing fights every day they never asked for. And that must stop.

I have chosen education as my life career focus, so I will approach celebrating personal learning and ending the "privilege monopoly" from that perspective in this book. I believe deeply that we must find ways to establish baseline levels of universal security in income, health, housing, and job opportunities. I am, however, arguing for something that runs even deeper. I am advocating for systemic structural and institutional respect and fairness for all.

And I am choosing higher education and lifelong learning as my focal points because I know the fields, and they are among the keys to breaking the monopoly on opportunity held by the privileged.

If unchecked, the privilege monopoly will ultimately destroy America. We must create levels of life security based on respect for other cultures and ways of life that bring everyone to the table of opportunity in a meaningful and substantial way.

So, that's my story. Now let's hear some others. I hope you appreciate and learn from them and embrace the lessons they convey for us all and for America.

Section 2: The Learning Journey

The Merry Go Round

These folks were constantly caught in an up-and-down, in and out experience with work, life, and college that left them dizzy and confused for years as they tried to sort things out. They are the epitome of people who were losing a fight that they never chose because that choice was determined at birth. But still, they found a way to jump off the merry-go-round and seize their future.

Rashaan Green

Rashaan Green is 34, and he lives in the Washington, DC metro area. He is working at Microsoft as a Principal Security Service Engineering Manager. He has a four-year-old chihuahua mix, plays video games, and helps others get into the Cyber Security field.

If there has been one consistent factor throughout my life, it has been coping with ADHD in a world that didn't understand it and respond effectively. I just learned differently. I went to therapy, took medication, the whole bit. But nothing really worked. I didn't realize it wasn't a disability to be corrected, i.e., something that needed to be fixed, until I was an adult. Now, I know that it is a different way of processing information.

Growing up in South Carolina, I was suspended from school multiple times because of ADHD. People just didn't know what to do with it or me as a result.

I really struggled with it, and I just didn't fit in. For example, I took a computer class in the ninth grade. They taught a specific method for typing, and I typed differently. My way was faster and more accurate. But the teacher wouldn't leave me alone. We got into an argument, and I walked out. I was in special ed classes, all sorts of different classes. Finally, I tried an alternative high school, but that didn't work either. So, my mom said it was either school or work and, at 16, I went to work.

I worked in two or three restaurants for the next couple of years. There was a guy who had been in one of them for 20 years, the head dishwasher. He told me that if I kept it up, I could be a head dishwasher too someday. I was freaked out! No way was that where I was headed. It was one of two experiences I had during my teen years that influenced me forever. The other was being told several times that I didn't fit in.

So, I began looking for alternatives when I was 18. And I knew I had to get out of South Carolina because there was much less opportunity there, especially for a skinny Black kid who didn't "fit in." I collected my wits and chose to go to Maryland. I sure didn't have anything to lose. I wanted to do something different with my life. I was 18, had worked in restaurants, and I wanted something better and different. It was the beginning of a search for a different future.

I reached out to my uncle, who lived in Maryland, because there was a Job Corps Center there, the Woodland Jobs Corps Center. I had researched several centers, and Woodland had computer-related training, which I craved. When I was a kid, I had been enrolled in a computer repair course in junior high school. But as I said earlier, I had to drop out. I loved computers, and I went to the library all the time because they had computers that I could play with. And my aunt lived near the Job Corps Center. So, off I went to Maryland. I enrolled at Woodland and got a job on the weekends at Chuck E Cheese. I was 18.

It was intense. I turned 18 in 2004, graduated from Woodland in 2005 with a certificate in computer repair and my GED, and got my first apartment. You had to have a job to graduate, and I had been hired as a data entry specialist at a sales company. A few months later, I was promoted to be an IT/helpdesk specialist. And I really liked that job because I was doing interpretive work. I stayed with that till 2007, when I decided to go back to South Carolina.

I wanted to go to college, but I had no idea how to do it or what was required. I first tried when I was in South Carolina in 2007, but that didn't work. It was a community college, and I was trying to balance full-time work with a full course load on campus. The schedule was impossible, and I dropped out.

About a year and a half later, I was working for Verizon, and they opened a call center in Atlanta. I applied for a job there, was accepted, and moved to Atlanta. Overall, I was there for five years. During that period of time, the economic collapse hit home, and I lost my job. I was unemployed and decided to try college again and better myself. I still failed, but this time I passed one class.

I had heard about Western Governors University from a friend at Verizon. I checked it out, and I really liked the fact that it allowed me to manage my own degree and pathway. I enrolled in their Business-Information Technology program in November 2011. I wasn't going to drop out again because, without the degree, you can never go further in your career. For example, if you do well at a role, the next level may be a management position, but it requires a degree.

But still, while I was going to WGU, things were tough. I was still stuck because I didn't have a degree. I got another job, a temp-to-perm job, but then my car broke down, and I needed another one. Then I lost that job, but I got another one. The problem was that the pay was way less. So, I am behind in rent. But I hung in there at WGU during this time. Despite the economic challenges, I was doing okay at WGU. I was struggling a little, still behind on some bills, but I had a job, and I was working and going to college from home.

Then, one morning I am getting ready to go to work, and my power was cut off. And that was that. I decided that I would go home to South Carolina. I put everything that would fit in my car and headed home. In reality, I was bankrupt, and I had to live at home with my mother. But you know, that really put a fire in my belly. There is something about living with your mother in your hometown that is something you don't want to do again.

While I was there, I began to focus on getting certifications through self-study. I got my Comptia A+ and Security + certificates in about 2.5 months. I was still at WGU as well. I identified a job at a company that had a contract at the local community college. I got the job and moved back to Maryland. My uncle had a place where I only needed to pay the utilities, and that allowed me to pay off my debts from Atlanta while working and going to school.

After years of trying to make a better life for myself, this was the beginning of the life I had dreamed of living. After a while, I got my own apartment, and then along came my second chance. I had applied for a job at the Johns Hopkins University Applied Physics Lab. I got my security clearance and a temporary contract position. That turned into a full-time job just two months before I graduated from WGU in 2014. Then I got promoted to a cybersecurity position, and that was the beginning of the rest of my life. I was working at the lab, I had my B.S., and I liked cybersecurity.

After a year, I wanted to get my master's degree. I tried WGU, but I was not qualified for the master's program in technology because it was a new program, and they required the CISSP certificate for admission. I didn't have it. So, I tried Capella, but that didn't work because there was not the flexibility in taking the classes that I loved and, as it turns out, that I needed to succeed due to my ADHD. I went back to WGU and, even though the door was still closed in Cyber Security, I enrolled in their Master's Program in Leadership. I needed to stay in college because I needed that next step up.

Then, I wrote to the Cyber Department's Program Manager. I wrote an email with my resume and my certifications and asked for entry into the program. They admitted me in February 2016.

Since graduation in April 2017, I left the Applied Physics Lab and went to Northrop-Grumman on a temporary contract. After six months, I got a permanent position and then was promoted to be Cyber Information Assurance Manager. But I moved again, and I am currently a Principal Security Service Engineering Manager at Microsoft. This is the dream job that I never quite believed I'd get.

Despite all my work experience knowledge and certificates, getting the BS changed everything. After that, whenever I applied for jobs, I was on the inside looking out because I had a degree. The certifications I had earned were very important. But the degree sealed the deal. It sets you apart from other candidates. I got interviews where I hadn't before.

The master's degree has a focus on things I actually couldn't do at work, like risk management. It actually put me ahead of the game. When Risk Management became a thing, I already knew how to do it. When I got that master's, my career took off.

But the learning model made the difference. Without WGU's approach, I wouldn't be where I am today. First, you managed your own time and progress. Second, they assigned every student a mentor, which was very effective. It was like having a partner, a project manager, for your studies and work. I had great relationships with my mentors, and they helped me navigate the University and my studies if I needed help there. In the master's program, and actually all programs at WGU, they allow you to use industry certifications as course credits, and they do other assessments of prior learning as well. Very cool.

My mom always said don't ever accept "no" for an answer, and I never have. When one door closes, another opens. And I learned a lot along the way. Like when I was unemployed in Atlanta and didn't have food to eat, I was seeing a therapist. She saw me for free, and she also bought me groceries from time to time. That taught me humility and empathy.

She encouraged me and said, "Remember that you will need to help others at some point when you are in a better position." I was in a place where no one else could help me. It came right down to the wire. All this led me to always think about other people. I carry that forward every day. She changed my life, and now I will try to help others.

Another thing. Along with the ADHD, race has been an issue at times. Leaving South Carolina, then going back there to live, and then leaving again was racially influenced. I wouldn't have had the same opportunities in the South that I had in the DC region and Maryland. The opportunities are just not the same. As a practical matter, that is just the way it is. Whether it is all about race or there is a shortage of opportunities as well, I can't say. But the consequence was the same.

When I think about my journey to date, I am thankful for everyone who believed in me, even when I didn't believe in myself. As you travel through the journey of trying to create the life you want, you will have challenges. But it's important to have a strong support system. I am living the life that I live today because my mother told me to never accept no for an answer; my aunt was there for me with a place to stay, and a therapist in Atlanta brought me food when I was broke!

I carry humility for others in my life every day because of all the experiences I have had to date. Today I have something that I spent years seeking, which is a career. Everything I had prior to obtaining my degrees was a job. And I learned so much coming up that ladder. But those jobs, and the learning I did on them, the certificates I got, were all steppingstones to help me get to where I am today. The degree redefined my life. My life to date is proof that, with patience and persistence, you can do anything you want to if you are willing to do the work.

Dinesha Monteiro

Dinesha is a single mother. At 25, she is a second-year student at College UnBound and Assistant Manager at a non-profit group home in Providence, Rhode Island.

It's hard to know where to start. My life has pretty much been a series of ricochets as events that were largely out of my control bounced me around. Neither of my parents went to college, nor did my three brothers. So that was the home environment I grew up in. I attended the Metropolitan Regional and Technical Center in Providence, graduating in 2013. Dennis Littke, the founder, and president of College UnBound (CU), founded it, and it had a very different learning philosophy than what I had experienced in the public schools.

The Community College of Rhode Island (CCRI) was next. But then there was a convergence of events at home which complicated my life incredibly and forced me to leave college. One of my older brothers was diagnosed with a seizure disorder. And my younger brother had been born with congestive heart failure and cardiomyopathy. That was the situation. Then my older brother shot himself in the head. He survived, but he lost an eye. And since he was technically disabled anyway with the grand mal seizures, he was not able to pitch in and help support the family. I know it was a bummer for him as well.

But all that combined to take me out of college and force me to get a job. First, I worked at a restaurant in Providence as a cashier and then on the cook line. I worked my way up through the different functions. Pretty quickly, I was at the supervisor level, though there weren't any fancy titles. We all just worked with each other. And I was there about four years. I lived in a studio apartment and went to work faithfully. But the notion of college was always there on the back burner.

Eventually, I went back to CCRI in their Social Work program, even though I had been in the General Education Program the first time. I had two jobs in addition to college, the restaurant, and then also at a furniture store. But, surprise, surprise, I became pregnant. So, I left the furniture store and CCRI again. Just no way to do it all. I stayed at the restaurant until two weeks before I gave birth. And I was back at it three months later.

Being a mother is amazing, if slightly stressful. My son was born a little over a month early, and that sort of pushed things forward. We ended up extending our stay at Woman and Infants Hospital due to the fact that my son had jaundice. Everything was taken care of, and I was beginning to learn how to balance everything. With the support of my immediate family, I was able to go back to work at the restaurant.

As I was working, I realized I wasn't fulfilling this fire in me. I wasn't doing what I wanted to do, nothing even remotely close. It was shortly after that I was blessed with the opportunity to interview for a job where the pay was slightly more, and there was actually room to grow in the company. The job was similar to what I thought I would love to be doing for a while, and so I went for it. I attempted to maintain a part-time position at the restaurant for a while, but then it all just became too much, and admittedly I needed change. I left the restaurant and began to pick up overtime at my new full-time job. About a year or so later, I was promoted, and maybe 6 months after that, I made assistant manager.

Today I am the Assistant Manager at a non-profit group home, an assisted living facility for adults. I tried again at CCRI, but that didn't work out. There were still way too many things to do, balls to juggle in a day. And college just didn't fit in with my work and my parenting. Something had to go, and it was college.

But then I took a leap of faith and tried College UnBound. A few months before leaving CCRI and transferring to CU, I connected with an old advisor who had assisted The MET students with college prep and other advice. She informed me that CU was children-friendly and worked around your schedule and recommended that I give it a go.

CU is based upon project work and people's passion. It makes your work part of the learning. Assuming what you're doing for work is a passion that you're living, you can utilize it and the skills you have and put them into your schoolwork. The program is truly based on your interests. It was a bit tricky for me because my project and my work had little to do with each other. But that was ok with them. I started my project off with the idea of maintaining self care. I came to this because a lot of people work and take care of the kids, the bills, and life and rarely have time for themselves. I was able to input my own struggles into this project.

But along the way, I have discovered a new passion that is directly tied to my experience as a single mother. My son will be four next year. But his father was incarcerated shortly after he was born. And that was, as they say, yet another complicating factor that put me in a bad situation in every respect. Then I met a single father, and I was really taken by the challenges he was facing. They were every bit as complicated as mine. But it appeared there were far fewer supports for him. So, my study at College Unbound (CU) is about single fathers. I love the people I work with. And, when my son's father gets out of jail, this study will help him.

Single parenting isn't just about the woman. I don't take any government assistance even though I could. So, my job is really important. But are single fathers offered the same financial and emotional support that is available to women? As part of my study, I have started a support group for single fathers. On a larger scope, I am hoping that I can shine a light on the needs of single fathers. So, I am giving back already.

As cliché as it might sound, I take it one day at a time. I learn hands-on. Both of my parents were sick with HIV, as well as my brothers having the issues I mentioned earlier. I coped with those situations and the pressures they generated and took care of myself, kept my life in order. There were roadblocks along the way because my brothers and my mother needed me.

But I gotta take care of myself first or I'll end up in the same jam they are in. It has taken time to find the right balance. I am still there for my mom. And my brothers are better, but still up and down. My project is a learning journey for me as well as the men in it. I am learning how to take care of myself at work as well as at home. My free time is kid, school, and work. That's it. I make the decision on a daily basis as to what I am going to do. How to juggle better is what I am trying to learn about in my support group.

Mom and aunt take care of my son when I am working. I am raising a pretty good kid, and that helps. Kids are a learning journey. I want more kids in the future. But I need to graduate and get a little more settled first.

I worked my way up in the current company, a public non-profit. I started up as a direct support professional. Then I got promoted to direct support specialist, leadership role, cross-training, it just kinda happened. Learn about the people and then personalize. My supervisor has been doing it for 16 years. She is very helpful, and she models the way to do the job for new staff. For her, no questions, no comments, and no concerns are out-of-bounds. She is a great mentor.

I have always kept growing and learning. I have been cross-trained at four different locations, the people, the differences, different disabilities, and medications. I work under the supervisory Nurse's license. And I became an assistant manager about two years ago.

There are a few people who have helped me succeed, including my mom and my Met high school advisor. She would call me out on my BS and help me see the path forward. And she is still supporting and mentoring me seven years later. My son's father has been very supportive as well. We are really good friends. He is still incarcerated. But we are working on what it will be like for him as a single father when he is released because that will be good for my son.

What has College UnBound meant? CU was an eye-opener. It is a helpful college program that puts the students first. They understand the needs of each individual student and try to implement it all in the learning curriculum. As a team, we are growing together collectively. There are lots of talented students here at CU ready to dive in with each individual project to help make a difference. I am glad to be a part of the CU community.

There is a massive amount of support from the cohort and the advisors – Jose is very supportive. They create a network of support, jobs, interviews. Dennis, the president, came to the exhibition where we show the work we have done for the last semester, the papers, and projects. That's all part of the curriculum. They give you feedback, tell you what worked and what needs improvement.

Currently, I am in my second year. They counted my credits from CCRI, and my previous work experience, using their Learning in Public (LIP) process that converts work experience to credit.

Although life may be tough and get in the way more than we would like, we are all given amazing opportunities daily, regardless of if we recognize that or not. We have to take the lessons we learn in strides. There are days we want to give up and end the fight. But something I tell everyone I know is to allow yourself to be helped, whatever it is you may need to help you get back on your feet. Support is always waiting somewhere close by.

Everything you have done in the past has gotten you to where you are, and that is intact prior learning. But, if you want to be specific, prior learning is something you learned, gathered, actually have done in the past that can and will be beneficial for the future. Somedays you may not feel like you've done anything, and that's okay. It is important to me that I talk to my support system and get the help I need for the situation I am in at that time. I will be the first to say that, at times, I can be my own worst enemy. I will self-sabotage and put myself down. But it is important to have people you can call that can pick you right back up when you're ready.

Susan Fenwick

Susan Fenwick is in her early 50s. She lives with her husband and their youngest child in western Washington, where she serves as HR and Operations Office Manager for a chain of 10 McDonald's restaurants.

For me, there are a million places I could begin. Let's start with the long view. I grew up in southern Oregon, Klamath Falls. I moved to be with my dad in Kirkland, Washington, after I left foster care at 16 because I had to team up with someone to survive.

High school was a complete disaster, a blur. I had people tell me I couldn't go to college. As a freshman, one teacher told me that I probably wouldn't graduate. He said, "one in five of you won't make it." By the time it was over, I had gone to five high schools, had been living on my own at 15, and in foster care when I was 16. Then I aged out and had to go back on my own.

I met my first husband at 18. He was at the local military base in Washington. When he got out of the service, we moved to Maryland. Then, after 2 years, we both knew we had made a mistake and decided to divorce. It was friendly, but there I was on my own in Maryland. And before I went back to Washington, I also lived in Ohio and Kentucky. Everywhere I went, I worked at McDonald's because I knew the ropes. You just walk in, show them you know your stuff, and they hire you.

Early Childhood Education or Physical Therapy would probably have been my professional goals if I had had access at 18. But my motivation was to pay rent and prove to people that I could do it; to succeed and be more than a burger flipper. I proved myself across multiple settings at McDonald's. By moving around, I learned at every place, and I could take what they were doing with me when I moved on. And that enlightened and strengthened the contributions I could make in future settings and jobs.

I moved back to Western Washington at 25 (1993) and started with the guy who is my current boss. I had to work up to it, but after a year, I was a General Manager. Then, in six months, he moved me to another store.

We moved with him to the Kitsap Peninsula in 1997. I was with him as a General Manager and then moved up to Area Supervisor for five restaurants. Had I not moved around previously, I wouldn't have had the diverse and extensive experience that I had accumulated along the way. But when I moved to Kitsap, I got it packaged. It was like I had made a million snowflakes. But over the next twenty years at Kitsap, I made a snowman.

Now let's do a little more detail. As a youngster, I didn't have a lot of opportunities or parenting, to put it mildly. Things were pretty rough on the home front in terms of money and attention. But I always had an inner voice that kept me out of trouble. And that inner voice kept me on a positive path for the first 16 years through thick and thin. But during my senior year in high school, everything collapsed.

My driving force at 15 was seeing what my five older brothers and sisters were doing and not doing the same things. I didn't want to do and be like them. In general, they were and have been an object lesson in failure, struggle, and wasted time throughout life in any way you can think of – alcohol, drugs, crime. I had to get away – the "push" was their example, the "pull" was proving myself. But college was never on the screen. No one had even thought about college.

Here I was, going to school, working, living independently, and having to care for younger siblings. When I moved to Washington at 16, I had aged out of foster care, and I needed an apartment. One of my older sisters had to sign the lease. Before that, I had been moving around among friends in Oregon. I was determined to graduate from high school. But just keeping up with schoolwork, as you can imagine, was an enormous problem.

At one point in my senior year, I was really behind on a bunch of assignments. I worked ferociously to finish them up. I literally worked every free minute for a week and a weekend. I got a bunch done, had it all in my backpack, and went to school. I got to school, put it in my locker, and took off to find my friends. When I got back to my locker, it had been broken into. My backpack had been stolen with my purse and all my work. I wasn't half as worried about the purse. But I was crazed about the homework. I searched all over the school, even in the dumpsters out back, but no homework. I couldn't find it anywhere. I went to the principal's office, and they helped me. But at the end of the day, no homework is no homework. I needed to do it again.

That was the breaking point. I walked out of the school and never looked back. At that point, I am just taking care of myself. I had been working at MacDonald's since I was 15, earning the minimum wage. What's sort of amazing about it is that this all happened in the early to mid-1980s. I've worked at McDonald's ever since then, and I've been with my current boss since 1993. Now I'm the HR manager for 10 stores. Quite a trip.

Along the way, I've done a little bit of everything because I was determined from the beginning to make something of this, precisely because I had no education. Yes, I worked in the restaurant. But there is more to the business than burgers, shakes, and fries, a lot more. On the front lines, beyond just doing the job, among other things, you need teamwork and a respect for diversity both on the team and in the customers. Also, I took all the training that was there, management classes, everything.

I met my husband, got married, and had kids, so that pushed education farther back. With four children who arrived with him and two more who we created over the years, life was busy! So, the focus had to be on work and kids.

Looking back now, I can see that I had been learning on the job since the very beginning. Over those years, I served on the crew and then as a crew manager. I had to pass verifications that I knew the positions because I was so young. Then they made me a shift manager by the time I was 17. By 1992, at 24, I was an assistant manager. I remember managing a shift one day, and it went smoothly, literally no problems. I remember walking out and saying, "I did that. Me, without a high school diploma, had a smooth shift, little waste, people got along, equipment worked, everyone working together."

In 1993, when I started with my current boss, I had to take a demotion to get in the door. But I quickly proved myself and moved up. A lot of my learning was on me. I kept asking how to do things, to soak up what they knew. Seeing the fruits of my labor and learning in real time was very powerful. I became an assistant manager and started at McDonald's' Hamburger U in Oakbrook, where I took all sorts of training classes in how to manage people, the books and money, operations, everything. I became a store manager in 1995. When I got my first promotion, my boss said, "Susan, you're going to be a great addition because you work well with people. "And here I am in HR with him 25 years later.

But my friends were still calling me "the flipper." In the 1990s, they said it all the time. There is this image that you are stupid, low income, and lazy if you work at McDonald's. It's that simple. But it's neither accurate nor fair. And frankly, I am very glad that I have that operational knowledge I gained from coming up through the system. Now, whenever someone comes to me with an issue, my answer is not hypothetical because I've been there. All that learning was not because of college. It was because of life experience.

In 2016, I finally finished high school through the Archways to Opportunity program. I was only the second of my eight brothers and sisters to do so. It was a real diploma, not a GED. I was 48 years old, and that was when I started looking for a college and a B.A. I got my B.A. in 2018 from Colorado Technical University. They have 88 online degrees, and they were partnered with McDonald's and Archways. They provided a free laptop, and the career counseling was awesome.

But listen to this. I got the degree in two years because my McDonald's' training was counted for academic credit. And then there was that other learning, learning about relationships with people and knowing how to work with different people- ethnicities, religion, age. I learned all that at McDonald's because there are all manner of people and motivations there.

I had to be able to learn how to buy into a consistent way of doing things, whether it is making a Big Mac or how to treat customers or whatever. I was working through other people. My success is based on their success and my ideals. With five restaurants, that's the only way to succeed.

So, they let me test out of courses, and I did that successfully in 18 courses! I probably would not have been as successful in college without the life and work experience. I was surprised because all the courses I took, even the ones I didn't test out of, felt familiar to me. It was like I had been in a tutorial for 25 years. I studied for the degree for 25-30 years, and that qualified me for two years of Advanced Placement. I knew it, and I could do it. In fact, I had done it already. So, the courses were frosting on the cake of my knowledge base.

In hindsight, my experience tells me that, while higher education may give you structure, build discipline and hold a whole slew of other benefits, the school of life can very well teach you everything you need to know to be successful. The real challenge is not burying yourself in student debt, so you have to find a high-paying job that you might or might not enjoy; a job that takes your time and commitment from your family and relationships, all in the name of "keeping up with the Jones's."

Instead, the goal should be to find something you can do that combines giving back to your community, helping others, building relationships, and providing for your family. If you can find something that helps others do the same while working with or for you, that's even better. I don't think you can completely learn that in a classroom or zoom meeting. And even if you learn some of it, you will still miss out on the learnings that come from the experiences and interactions of life. To me, those are the lessons that you carry with you. The lessons that help you to make decisions and find solutions. You need to live it to know it.

My time with McDonald's is almost up. The Franchisee Operator I have been with for over 25 years will be retiring soon, and I want to do more. I'm not ready to retire. McDonald's as a system has been here for me for a majority of the years in my life. I was raised under the arches. Archways to Opportunity made it so I could accomplish obtaining a B.A., something I always wanted but didn't think was within my reach. I thought I needed it to prove something to the world. I realize now I did not need it. I needed what my experiences taught me. I am incredibly grateful to McDonald's and the Archways to Opportunity program. I look at it as the final hoo-rah and thank you for my years of service and dedication. It is a bucket list accomplishment that I am extremely proud of. However, it did not provide what I thought it would. Life did that.

From here, I will probably look for another job in HR. I am taking the SHRM Certificate test soon, and then I'll start looking for another job. I also plan to continue to work with local high schools and other programs for youth and adults as well. It is an incredibly exciting thought that I might help someone who is just like I was that first day of my freshman year in high school when the principal told me I would probably not graduate from high school, let alone go to college. Something in me broke that day. And it took me 35-40 years to fix it but fix it I did!

I want to help them understand that if higher education is what they want, they should not let anyone tell them they can't have or get it. More than that, I hope to be an influence to help others understand that if higher education is not what they want for whatever reason, they are still worthy of a fulfilling life. They absolutely can learn outside of a classroom or zoom meeting in our current world.

A degree definitely has benefits, but those benefits are not required to help others or to define them or their status in life. Although a degree is not required to build a life as a happy, healthy, productive member of society, it can give you confidence. My point is degree or no degree…you can make a difference in someone's life. Degree or no degree…you are able. Choose what's best for you without preconception about what is socially dictated as appropriate and necessary.

Dreams Deferred: One Step at a Time

These people were as determined and resolute as they were frustrated. But they let life unfold and seized opportunities when they arose, finally getting to a better future for them and their families.

Susan Johnson

Susan Johnson is a Sales Associate at Walmart in Del Rio, Texas.

Three things have defined my life up to the current day: I have been working since I was 13 years old; I have been under medication since I was 24 from untreated scoliosis; and I have a relationship with my husband where we have always picked each other up and kept on moving, no matter what the problem.

Because of numbers one and two, I haven't been able to do a lot of what I might have liked to do for most of my life. Like a lot of other people, I've done what I had to do. No choice. But 98% of my time has been spent on the "must-do's." Sometimes you just have to bite the bullet. So, my life has largely consisted of tough choices. And I have had to be very tough, a tough chick. If you worked with me, you'd call me "nice." But the people who know me, they crack up when I am described as nice.

I think a lot of it has to do with being raised in the military. Being an Air Force brat was a unique experience. When you have lived in six places—Michigan, Louisiana, Pakistan, Texas, Alaska, and New Mexico—by the time you are 21, it has a big impact on you. My dad was an enlisted man, rose to Senior Master Sergeant over his 28-year career, and I was just following him around. You live in a sharply defined world, but you are moving all around the country and overseas. New friends, no friends, old friends. The cycle kept repeating itself. The military is its' own culture. You grow up very differently in the military. And it's military, military, military all the time.

For example, I was in Pakistan as a young kid, and it changed my life. The situation there was like being isolated in a foreign world. My school was on the base like any other, but we lived off the base. And living in the Pakistani population was an entirely different experience, say, than in a neighborhood in Michigan or even on a military base in Texas. By the time I was ten, I knew what war was, what the slave trade was, what poverty was, and what a different culture was. And I knew what fear was because we actually had to come home when things got ugly.

But with all the moving around, there was one constant. I started working at 13, and I've been working ever since. At 14, I was a Red Cross volunteer on the Male Orthopedic Ward at Wilford Hall Medical Center in Texas. You say that and some people think, "Oh, you were a candy striper." No, I worked in the wards and performed the services that a certified Nurses Aide would do today. I took temperatures and blood pressure, changed clothes and bedpans, you name it.

In high school, I was in a program called health occupations. It was vocational in nature, and I was in school 50% of the time and working in the field the other 50%. The idea is that you would practice every day doing the job that you are being taught at school. That was a very different life from the other students, to put it mildly.

When I first started in the program, I wanted to be a dietician. And I was thinking about a B.A. because I needed the degree to do that. And since I was the only one aiming for dietician, they created a special program just for me. And that put me in a supervisory role on Day One. So, responsibility came quickly. But by the time I turned 18, I had been working for five years, and I was sick and tired of school. I wanted to get away from it badly. So, at that time, college was the furthest thing from my mind. I figured that I didn't need college.

Age 20 was a huge turning point for me. We were in Alaska. My dad had gotten shipped to Elmendorf Air Force Base in Anchorage and I, at age 17, went with the family. My dad had compelled me to do this because I was still 17, and he was in charge. I got a volunteer job in the air force health facility and also worked downtown at the Providence Hospital in Anchorage. Although I didn't see it clearly at the time, I was moving away from the medical focus because I was burned out by the pain and suffering that I was exposed to every day.

The actual turning point came when I was working with a six-year-old girl whose parents had thrown her into a bonfire when she was three. There she was, still wrapped in bandages and suffering after almost three years. And just being with her broke me. It was the last straw. So, I very quickly got a second, part-time job as an exercise instructor teaching aerobics. And that move away from health care towards exercise and management was a big one for me.

Then, when I was 20, my dad was transferred to Albuquerque. This was a really, really tough move for me. Having moved so much, I was sick of that. And I loved Alaska, the mountains, and the ocean. But I didn't have the money to live alone in Alaska, and I was still a military dependent. So, my plan was to move to New Mexico, get a job, and make enough money to return to Alaska.

But it was at this point that my health became a major, ongoing factor in my life. Towards the end of my time in Alaska, I had been diagnosed (a late diagnosis) with scoliosis after I herniated a disc. I had been suffering from back issues for years, and there was no way I was going to have an operation on my back, having seen the consequences of back surgery in hospitals. I knew that, at some point, my back would give out, but what was I going to do?

It turned out that Albuquerque was a real turning point for me. I was there for 20 years. I worked multiple jobs, met my husband, OJ, and got married, and taught at the University of New Mexico continuing education program, among other things. I was always on the move. First, I got a job in a health spa as a service director. I supervised all the instructors and the exercise programs at 21. I was shifting away from "helping" to "healing"—away from the hospital and getting to people before they needed formal help. It was intense and, as you may have determined by now, so was I. I worked all the time. After about four years, my body broke down. This time I had more than one herniated disc, and I literally had to crawl to my car. I wanted to be the best, and I drove myself relentlessly, but then my body gave out.

Over the next few years, as the pain came and went, I used a cane, rehabbed myself, took prescribed medicine, and used alcohol as well to cover the pain. The ongoing expense of the medical treatment, combined with the lack of mobility and ongoing pain and anxiety, were factors in my life. But ongoing exercise and taking good care of myself have made all the difference over the years. Having said that, I learned something important during this period as well. I was in physical therapy one day. It was painful, and I was crying. I said, "I can't do this anymore!" And the therapist, looking at me directly, said, "You're not dying. Let's get going!" I realized she was right, sucked it up, and kept going. And that is the way it has been ever since. The hardest thing I ever heard was also the best thing I ever heard.

After my career in exercise and spas ended, thanks to my failing body, I went to bartending school, got a job in a bar, and that was my course for the next six years. I quickly became a supervisor. I continued to suffer from health issues. But I was working because I needed to make money.

My experience as a manager/leader had been accumulating for 15 years, ever since I worked in that Texas hospital as a junior volunteer. My experiences made me stronger and better than others my age. I was very aware of my experience as a leader. I knew how different it made me. I knew who to talk to and what to say in order to get the leadership job that was available. At the bar, I was there full-time, with no kids, no other distractions. I really liked focusing on work. I had three foci in life-work, personal health, and having fun. Then I met my husband-to-be and, after living together in Albuquerque for three years, we were married.

In my thirties, I didn't have to work because he was working, and I was a housewife, a stay-at-home mom. I loved sewing, and I did a lot of sewing. Then, following that passion, I got a part-time job at a fabric store, Hancock Fabrics. After three weeks, they asked me to become the Assistant Manager, and I accepted. And a little while later, I opened my own business on the side. It was an upholstery business named CoverUps. Then, I went for the trifecta and began teaching classes at the University of New Mexico continuing education program.

I was still at Hancock Fabrics. I talked them into supplying a couple of rooms in the back of the building, and I turned them into classrooms. The deal was that the university got the rooms for nothing. Hancock had potential customers walking through the store to attend my classes in "How to Reupholster Furniture" and "Making custom-fitted slipcovers," and I was making money from both. I was working, running my own business, and teaching. It was sweet.

The '90s, however, turned into a tough time for us. Hancock, the focus of my trifecta, went out of business. So, I had no place to teach and no "outside" job. During the same period of time, the University of New Mexico decided that people working in their technology department had to have a B.A. to qualify. My husband had some pertinent college, and he was self-taught, but he didn't have a degree. So, that was that. He decided to become a real estate agent. Although we thought we had planned this transition carefully, things didn't work out at all. Ultimately, we went bankrupt and lost our house, but we took care of everything and put our financial problems behind us.

We finally left New Mexico in 2001. OJ and I had visited Traverse City in Michigan in the early 2000's to connect with my remaining grandparent. He fell in love with the place, and I had loved it since I lived there during my childhood. We made a five-year plan to move, but it actually took us seven years to do it.

When we got to Michigan, he got a job, and I worked out of the house doing the same business as I had in Texas. But disaster struck again. We were heating with wood because it was cheaper, and we were short on money. It was wintertime in Michigan, and we had a chimney fire. We had no money, and we went two days without heat. But then bad luck struck again. We had purchased our house with a side agreement on a five-year balloon payment that would be extended without condition. But the 2007-2008 housing bubble hit, and the terms were changed. We went bankrupt again. That triggered a series of events that helped us cut back while still following our dream to be in Michigan.

The next few years went pretty smoothly. In 2011, we were both working and making decent money. And I was scheduled for a job interview at the Grand Traverse Resort. It would have been my dream job. But then my father underwent cancer surgery and, the next day, had a quadruple bypass. The doctors gave him two years. The same week, believe it or not, my husband's mother fell and hit her head. She slipped into a coma and died seven days later on New Year's Day. When my husband got back from the funeral, he said, "It's time for us to go home. I don't want you to go through what I just did." So, we packed our bags, quit our jobs, and scheduled the move. Ironically, we actually left for Texas, leaving our dream life behind, in the middle of a devastating ice storm.

As traumatic and disappointing as it all was, this was really the beginning of the next chapter of my life. I'd had 35 jobs in 39 years. Often I was working multiple jobs at the same time. And the supervising positions I had were not highly paid because they were largely at local and service-oriented businesses. I've done a lot of different jobs, from disc jockey to greenskeeper to bartender to fabric store supervisor. But the money was never there, and I didn't have the degree.

I landed a low-paying job at Dollar General in Del Rio. I told my boss about my experience and personal situation and that I couldn't afford to stay at that level. So, she helped me look at options. Dollar General had a University of Phoenix scholarship.

I applied, but I didn't get it. That was the downside. The upside was that I had to get three letters from prior employers for my application. And I was stunned and blown away by the show of support that came through those letters. I really had never thought about my abilities from an arms' length perspective, about what other people saw in me and my performance. To me, it just sort of "was what it was." But now, these former supervisors were praising my capabilities, and I began to reassess just who I was looking at in the mirror each morning and what expectations I could have.

So, even though I didn't get the scholarship, I went searching for another school. I knew what I knew, and I wanted to move up and make money. I had the skills but not the credential. I applied to then-Kaplan, now Purdue Global, got accepted, and went into the BS in management program.

I was shocked at the difference my experience made in the classes at Kaplan-Purdue. In the beginning, I was scared to death. Was I supposed to be there at all? And my husband just said, "We'll make this happen." And although it didn't make the work easier, all that prior experience gave me a huge edge in class. In my second year, I was invited to join the Honors Society (NSCS). Then, in my third year, I got a scholarship because of the Honors Society and landed an internship at Walmart. So, I quit my job at Dollar General and moved to Houston for three months. I've been with Walmart ever since.

To sum it all up, in spite of the chronic pain from my scoliosis, my 30-plus years of experience, along with my husband's support, were the differentiating factors in my success in school. Joining the Honors Society was the turning point. It was like a brand. But beyond that, the simple fact of going to college and succeeding made tangible and real all of what I knew and was able to do. I had "the right stuff," but without the degree, no one cared about it.

I've been a survivor all my life. I've always said I don't believe in do-overs. But if I could change one thing, I would go to college when I was younger. There are so many things that improve when you go to college that I know there would have been a different path. My new passion in life is getting people to further their education. It's not about the piece of paper. It's about the person you can become as a result.

My jobs have always been the means, not the end. I have learned a lot in my more than 35 jobs, both from positive advice, experience gained, and from negative treatment. You can learn from the negative, even if you don't like it. And I have done that.

Right now, I am learning Spanish. Del Rio, Texas, is on the border. Eighty-four percent of the population is Mexican. The majority language is Spanish. And I have decided that if I am going to work and live here, be a manager here – being bi-lingual is essential. When you are on the border and you are immersed in the Mexican culture, it is a whole different thing than Albuquerque, Dallas, San Antonio, or El Paso.

It is rural, and the sister city—Ciudad Acuna—is across the border. People commute back and forth every day.

At heart, as a manager, I am a teacher, an instructor, and I know how to work. So, I want to start a city-wide program teaching kids what it takes to be successful at work. When I knew that for myself, that's when I saw that I needed the degree, among other things. And that's why I am learning Spanish. When I am sufficiently fluent, I will then start this next big venture.

Like I said before, the job at Walmart and the degree from Purdue Global took everything I knew and turned it into something of tangible value. I toughed it out for almost 50 years, just gutted through the pain and the failures, and now I feel as if I am finally in charge of my life. Here's a funny story that I'll finish with. I remember one time when I was at a company meeting. When I told them about all the jobs I'd had, this one guy said, "And we hired this person?" I said, "Everyone hires me." The natural talent was always there.

Sarah Aronack

Sarah, the single mother of two, is the Occupational Health Manager for JBS/Pilgrims in Alabama.

I was born at Ellsworth AFB in South Dakota and grew up in Rapid City. My parents had grown up on the base and lived across the street from each other as kids. And they stayed there for their entire life. I was born in 1979, and Dad was still in high school. Mom had graduated and was working as a switchboard operator. They were married three months after I was born.

Neither of them went to college, though they were very smart. Theirs was another story. They had a baby and went to work. Dad worked for the same company for 29 years, and now he works for the city. My mom works at the hospital as a program coordinator in the Family Medicine residency. She has no degree, and she actually started in an entry-level position at an insurance company many years ago. Then she went to the hospital as an administrative assistant when I was about 10. Since then, she has simply worked her way up the ladder based on determination and performance. Talk about live and learn!

So, I grew up in Rapid City and graduated from high school a year early. It wasn't that I was such a hot student. Actually, I didn't like school that much and wanted to get the hell out of there! I joined the Army National Guard and went to basic training. I handled that really well, and when I came home, I enrolled in the local college, Black Hills State/University of South Dakota.

But It just wasn't for me. There were two big problems. First, I didn't know what I wanted to do with my life. And second, the way the college curriculum was organized and delivered just wasn't for me. I am a competitor, and I like to *do* things. All through high school, I played basketball and soccer. And I learned a ton about teamwork and leadership, and tenacity during those years. So, when it came to college, I wanted hands-on action, not sitting in a room listening to someone talk. So, I decided to take a break until I could figure out what I actually wanted to do.

My parents didn't know how to help me because they didn't have any experience with college. As a family, we had enough, but we didn't have a lot. And they wanted me to have a different path. But I was the oldest child, so everything was the first time, an experiment, trial, and error. And, although my mother was very clear that she didn't want me to follow in her footsteps, she didn't know how to advise me on good alternatives and other career directions.

Working hard has never been the problem. I have worked since I was 15. After leaving college, I left for some more training in the military. I had always been drawn to the military. My family is full of people that have served, and it is something I grew up around. I also saw it as a way to pay for college. My parents had been very clear they would help as much as possible, but they could not and would not finance a degree. But when I came back the second time, I wanted to live on my own. My mom told me, "Ok, but you have to support yourself." She suggested that I apply at the hospital she works for. So, I did, and I got a job in the emergency room as a clerk. Then I enrolled in college for the second time. But that didn't work any better than the first time.

So, now I am through with the college thing. I felt like I had failed at school and would never finish anyway. I didn't know what I wanted to do. I had floated around and searched, but I never found the prize. Then it happened for me, as a late bloomer when I fell in love with healthcare. The Emergency Room job was a real eye-opener. I discovered that I loved hands-on, health-related activities! One day I met an older woman at work. She was an LPN, and she told me about a local LPN program that was one year long. So, I applied, and along came college number three. I got in, I loved it, and I was successful. I graduated at the top of my class. The Voc-Tech nature, hands-on, was what I loved. I was 21 when I graduated.

I worked for a while and ultimately decided that I wanted to get out of town. So, I went on active duty in the Army. During those years, I encountered people with more credentials than I had but who lacked the ability to perform, especially in high-pressure settings. Here I was, an LPN, showing RNs how to do their jobs, and in some cases doing their jobs for them! I was explaining stuff to people that they should have already known. It was difficult, given the army structure, that they were a level above me, getting paid more, and they didn't know what was going on.

After I left the service, I worked as an LPN in Kentucky. And one day, it came to me, and I thought, "This is nuts. I am doing their work and earning one half to one-third of what they earn." That was the kick in the pants that got me going, once and for all, on the education track. In the next few years, I got my Associates Degree and BS in Nursing while still working full-time. Along the way, I got married to a guy in the service. We moved to Texas when he was transferred. When we moved, I picked up my B.A.-Nursing program and transferred it to a college in Texas.

What was really frustrating was that I had to repeat courses at my new school because they wouldn't accept the credit from my college in Kentucky. I mean, how many times do you have to take Psych 101? So I lost a lot of credit when we moved. It cost me time and money, but I didn't let it turn me off.

I had gone from being a service member to being at the mercy of my husband's service obligation, and that in itself was a transition for me. He had multiple deployments as well, which made a complex schedule worse. I felt guilty being away at school when he was home because we were always getting ready for him to leave again. Or he would get his mid-tour leave to come home for two weeks, and I was trying to figure out how to take a final exam and pick him up from the airport at the same time. So, while I finally had the motivation for school, I felt I was constantly having to pick and choose between it and everything else. It was stressful.

I was always working full-time when I was going to school. The only exception was when I had my sons. For both my associate's and bachelor's degrees, I had to finish my degree work in a hurry before I had my baby. At one point, I was literally in labor, trying to hurry and submit a final project for a class. Then in each case, I took three months off and went back to work. It took a lot of scheduling and dexterity. It was after my second son was born that I enrolled in Western Governors University's Masters in Nursing Leadership and Management. That was when I learned how to breastfeed holding the baby in one hand and typing with the other while keeping a two-year-old entertained, all at the same time.

WGU was self-paced. If you are a motivated person, you can get it done quite quickly. One class I finished in a week. If you know the content, you can take the evaluation whenever you were ready. Some other classes took me three to four weeks. So, as I had understood it, I needed the B.A. from an accredited University, but then the master's was sort of an extra. I didn't want to sit in class for another two years, so the flexible WGU approach was perfect for me. And you know what? I learned more in that program than I did in the previous two.

Every time I look back on things, the motivation was that I was doing the work of others and not getting paid for it. They were making more and treating me without respect, while I knew more and could do better. So, getting the RN was really a confirmation for me, and it gave me a brand that advertised my capacity. And, ironically, I had thought that I was getting my MSN to support my first husband after he left the service. But we got divorced, and it ended up supporting me.

I have been living in Alabama for seven years, since before the divorce. I'm now enrolled in The University of Alabama Nursing Capstone Program and am projected to graduate from the Family Nurse Practitioner Program in 2022. It's going to be a hectic experience once again since I will be working full time and a single mom of seven- and nine-year-old boys. But it will be worth it. Maybe by experiencing it with me, I can teach them a fraction of what my parents taught me about hard work and determination. Ultimately, I'll go after my Doctorate.

Once I found my passion and an approach to learning that suited me, I did just fine. And most of it as a single parent!

Ultimately, I want my experience and journey to serve as motivation to others that have not taken the traditional route in terms of their career and education. College is not for everyone, and there should be no shame if it isn't the right fit for you. I felt like a failure for so long because of it when, in reality, that wasn't the case at all. And while my parents may not have had the familiarity to help me navigate the college system (which would not have changed the outcome for me at all), the things that they instilled in me on a basic level are what have ultimately made me successful. Strong work ethic, determination, honesty, leading by example, and the fact you have to work hard for the things you want are the most important lessons I ever learned. And those came from my parents, not from college.

My path has been very non-traditional. People often told me I was crazy or that I wouldn't succeed. And my life has taken turns I didn't expect it ever would. I just had to find a way to turn the negativity into motivation, and that is something I continue to do moving forward. I don't want sympathy or praise for my failures or accomplishments. I just want to make my kids proud and serve as an example to them like my parents have for me.

Heather Lumsden

Heather Lumsden is the mother of two daughters and lives in Greensboro Bend, Vermont. She is a human services worker for the state of Vermont.

I was born in Greensboro and have lived here, essentially, all my life. When I went to college, I had absolutely no idea what I wanted to do with my life. It was a classic case. I partied and, as they say, explored life. I had no focus. Then there was some financial trouble at home, and my parents couldn't afford the out-of-state tuition, so I came home and went to Trinity College in Burlington. That was a hard move for me. I was coming back home from a more independent and "away" experience. But I didn't take it seriously and didn't change my behavior. I got pregnant that summer and had a bi-racial daughter. So, I had to quit school and go to work. The next year I wanted to try and connect with my daughter's father in New York City. So, I moved there and tried to attend school part-time at LaGuardia Community College studying Human Services.

But my life was still totally unsettled and without focus. I left New York and the father of my daughter and came back to Vermont. Then I began to settle down a little. I mean, I had to take care of this little girl. So, first, I had a couple of little jobs. I delivered newspapers, worked at a deli, stuff like that. But then I got a job at the Cabot Creamery, a big dairy co-op near Greensboro. I really liked it there, and I moved up quickly and got into quality management.

I was at Cabot and happy to be there for over five years. Towards the end of that time, though, I got sick. Now I know it was Lyme's disease, but at the time I had no clue. Ultimately, I just couldn't do eight hours a day. So, I had to look for alternative options that were more appropriate given my physical issues. I got a Vocational Rehabilitation counselor who helped me find a job that I could do physically.

I was tending towards Human Services at that point. And I got a job at Washington County Mental Health Services. I was what they called a dialectical behavioral support staff, and I was working with a client who swallowed foreign objects to relieve tension. It was a whole new experience because it made me really use my brain, and there was the connection between brain and emotion. I did this for three to four months, and then I became a support manager and did that job for about three years.

Then a whole bunch of stuff happened at roughly the same time. I had another daughter and had to take maternity leave. And my client went into the state hospital, so there was nothing there for me when I returned. But I adjusted again and became a case manager for people who were at home with developmental delays.

I continued as a case manager there and stayed for about ten years. But they were filled with turmoil and a bad experience. I was harassed by my supervisor and, even though I brought in lawyers, I was demoted. So, ultimately, I left and found the family center where I currently work. Compared to working with adults with disabilities, this was a lot less wearing and more fulfilling as well. At the same time, I had to learn a lot. I was working with little kids and, although I was familiar with case management, I was not deeply knowledgeable in child development.

I've been bouncing around for my entire working life. I must work to protect and feed my kids. And I did well and moved up in virtually every job I had. I sort of learned like a sponge, soaking stuff up wherever I was. But there was no protection like a degree would give me, so I was always on the edge, it felt like.

Then, it happened again. My position was eliminated. They had a new organizational plan which required everyone to become developmental educators and do the required paperwork that went with the job. The new position required a B.A., and so I had a choice to make. Am I going to keep bouncing around, or am I going to bite the bullet? I decided to stay put and get the degree.

As I look back on it, at that point, Lyme disease was a big part of why I chose Human services ultimately instead of staying in management at Cabot. I needed something that was less physically stressful. But I also needed a new job that paid as much as what I was making. So, in the years since then, I have taken jobs where I can make my own pace and deal with it in a consistent manner, manage it. Flexibility is key.

I work well with people, and I am approachable. And I am curious about people, their behavior, and their nature. I am dependable and hard-working. And even though I bombed in college a couple of times, I have an urge to learn, and I learn every day.

So, with all these things in mind, I decided to bite the bullet and get the B.A. that they said I had to have. I had considered the Community College of Vermont in the past, but I didn't pursue it. Then came the directive, and I had to do it. I had already had a job that required a degree, case management, at Washington County Mental Health Services. They knew I could do it, so they grandfathered me in. That was when I first considered really getting the degree. But I wasn't offered any assistance, and my oldest daughter was going off to college, and I needed to support her. So, I didn't pursue it then.

But this time, it was different. My daughter was finishing school when the change came. As I said, the Family Center of Washington County wanted to give me a lower job, but I talked them into a plan that included my getting a degree. And the State—children's integrated services—was offering flexibility in getting the degree. But I had to give them a plan.

I've been in the process for a year. And I am beginning to see how it might work. One problem was that I had so many credits from so many different sources that it was hard to make sense out of it all. What did I have versus what did I need? This was all about being practical, no romance, just get it done. And it didn't have much to do with what I needed to learn. It was more about the courses I needed to take to fill in the blanks for the degree.

But figuring that out was a big deal. They had an Assessment of Prior Learning course that was a big help. It helped me organize the knowledge I had so that I could plan my future learning for the degree. I was amazed and very proud that I got so much recognition and validation for the knowledge I had from both other colleges and from my working and life experiences. It was interesting to see it all in one place. Even though I didn't have a college education, it was really validating and boosted my confidence. Everyone I asked to comment on my abilities was very helpful. I would recommend the assessment course to anyone. It saved me a lot of money, validated my life and work experience, and I got a degree plan put together as well.

This class saved me more than $20,000 in tuition fees and several years of classes since I can only manage a class or two each semester while working full-time and being a single mom. The course has given me hope and confidence in myself. Getting a B.A. will give me security in my life for continuing to financially support my family. I may even pursue further education after it now that I know I can do it!

As I am looking at colleges for the B.A., some are skeptical about awarding me credit for the APL plan. But that's a non-starter. I know the stuff, so I want advanced standing for it. And personally, I want to get it done before my daughter finishes school.

Professionally, I want the flexibility to move up and the freedom to move to another job if I want to. It gives me a lot more security. So, while I don't know what the future will bring, I know that with the degree and my experience, I'll be ready for anything.

Kalimah Shabazz

Kalimah Shabazz is a Veteran and a single mother of two. She lives in Arlington, Texas, and works for the federal government.

I was born in Oakland, but we moved when I was very young to North Carolina. We lived there till 1990, when my dad passed away, and then we moved to Kansas City. I am smart, but school has always been boring to me. It just didn't interest me, and I didn't see the point. I felt like mom didn't really push me, and there wasn't any other incentive to do well. As a result, I was held back twice in North Carolina, once in elementary school and again in the seventh grade. But once I was in Kansas City, they put me into the ninth grade. So, for the record, I did seventh grade twice and skipped eighth grade altogether. A little weird, but that was what happened when I came into that school in Kansas City.

When my dad passed, I had decided to try harder, and that was the attitude I took with me to Kansas City. They put me in a special program for kids who had been "pushed up" like me, and, surprise, surprise, I made the honor roll. I got honors in the 10th grade as well. But I never found school interesting, and after a while, my commitment to try harder sort of went away. I was just doing enough to make it, and my mom was doing the best she could. But I had Dad's independent streak, a love for boys, and I was going to do it my way. That was the way it was. In my senior year, I took a cooking class and got a certification for it. I love cooking, and that has never changed. But I wasn't going to do it for a living because I didn't want to stand up all the time.

During my senior year, I had some other ideas about careers. I was thinking about either going into the Army or being a stripper. I really wanted to be independent, but I couldn't do the stripping because I couldn't take my clothes off in public. (She laughs.) So, I joined the Army. That got me out of the house. And I had a paycheck, my independence, and three squares a day. Like I said, I am a lot like my dad. I like to be on my own—independent and on my own. I was 19. Ironically, I followed in his footsteps because I left home and joined the Army shortly after high school, just like he did.

I was stationed at Fort Bragg in North Carolina. Initially, I was an Ammunition Supply Specialist. But then I wanted to change into a different job, personnel administration or what is now known as Army HR. I had to raise my GT score in order to qualify for changing my job. So, I took a course that focused on the skills needed to raise my score—math, English, and so on. Then I took the test and met the objective, and went into Army HR. So, like I said, when it matters, I like to finish what I start.

When I got the new Army job, I transferred to Fort Meade. I had my first child when I was 24. I was engaged to the father, and we broke up during the pregnancy. But my community—civilians, Army people, and actual family—was very supportive. They really helped. I was in an apartment with a roommate. When the baby came along, we were a family of three. I liked the community and decided at that point to stay in Maryland. Also, his dad was in Virginia. So that was nearby.

But then the Army wanted to transfer me, and I said "no." That meant that I had to get out. And I needed a change. So, I moved to Atlanta, where I had friends. I moved on 9/11, believe it or not. But the whole thing was a disaster. I had job offers when I went, but nothing was signed, and the offers were withdrawn right after I got there, thanks to 9/11.

I wanted to go back to school, and I had the GI Bill. So, I did it with the goal of studying computer science. But I picked a garbage school. The TV ads were great, but the program was terrible. And I got sideways with the terms of my GI Bill support, and the money didn't come through. I had to drop out. Frankly, most of the problems were a result of no guidance. I was flying blind, and I made mistakes.

Over the next year, my car was repossessed, I got evicted because somebody stole my rent, and all I had was child support. I got a job at Waffle House, but it didn't pay enough to survive along with daycare and other living costs. We were very poor. Sometimes I ate nothing so my son could eat. Frankly, the whole experience was a blessing in disguise. I had to go through it to appreciate what I had achieved before. As a result, I re-upped into the Army.

I was in the National Guard the whole time I was in Atlanta. They helped me out by giving me a job during the week because I was broke. They were family to me. Let me bring my son in from time to time. This, along with the Waffle House gig, allowed me to survive. But I was making no money. Then I took a Physical Fitness test, and they asked me to go to a military school for three weeks. I got a certificate in leadership while getting paid at the same time. So, I had a leg up on things, and when I re-enlisted and I could concentrate on my former field —ammunition supply.

It was 2003. I was an E-5 Sergeant. After a month or so, I got orders to go to Germany. So, I moved to Germany, and my son stayed with my aunt in Arkansas until I got settled. I got there in May, and my son Rashawn got there in the late fall.

I was 27. It was the beginning of a fairly stable period in my life which lasted about 15 years through 2018. I made my home in the Army, picked up friends wherever I went. I was super-blessed, didn't miss any military movements. And I had learned something. When I needed help, I asked for it.

I had a new lease on life, and that was when I started with UMUC, now UMGC. I started with a little one-credit weekend class. It was pretty easy for me. I took four to five weekend classes like that, a credit apiece, and passed them all. Then I decided to take some regular courses. That was going okay, but then I took an English course, and I struggled. Although I love reading, I had always had trouble writing. I failed the class and took a hiatus from school. That was right around the time around the time my daughter was born. So, things were complicated and busy.

When my daughter came along in 2005, I had to learn how to care for two kids. When I was away from them, I was sad. But their dads took care of them when I was away, and I could use that time productively on school. The opportunity was terrific. UMGC was always there, wherever I was, and it was Army-approved. The online technology made the difference. Anytime, anyplace.

In 2006, I returned to the states. Eighteen months later, I was transferred to Korea, then back to the states and then deployed to Afghanistan and Kosovo. Most of the time, my kids were being cared for by their fathers. Other times by my mother. When I was in Kosovo, I really got serious and focused. I was on a mission that didn't take all day, so I had the time to study. I took about six classes and passed them all, including English! After Kosovo, I stayed with it and finished in 13 months.

Due to many bumps and bruises throughout my career, I had gotten to a point where I could no longer serve. I knew the end was coming when I got to my last duty station in 2017, Ft. Bragg, after Hawaii, and I had trouble getting out of bed every day. So, at that point, I was medically retired. It was mainly my back and knee-related. I had to have knee surgery which closed the door on my going to the next level. But in the end, I wear the term "disabled Veteran" proudly.

I retired in September 2018 and graduated in 2019 with a B.A. in Human Resources management after 16 years of studying, traveling, and raising my kids. The VA Voc-Rehab money put me over the top. I ended my career as a E-7, Sergeant First Class.

I was in North Carolina, and I waited to move to Texas until my daughter graduated from Middle School in Fayetteville, and I got my son situated at Fayetteville State University. He is a Music major! During this time, I worked as an Apprenticeship Counselor for a company that was serving military people who were transitioning out. Although I continued in that job until September 2020, I moved to Arlington, Texas in July.

I am just starting my Federal Career as secretary for the Director of the Commissary on the Naval Reserve Base. I will be doing human resources and logistics, among other things. Ultimately, I want to move into more HR-related work. I am stubborn and a born persister.

Despite all the setbacks and some bad luck, and poor decisions, I always had a plan. I try to take one step at a time towards the larger design, and I'll do what I need to do to succeed and do better. In life, I need to balance money and fulfillment. I need to be around people and interact with them. So, this is the beginning of a new stage. We'll see what happens.

As I look back on it all, me being a parent was what kept me focused and driving towards my goals. I fumbled a little bit, but I kept focused on doing the right thing and being a good example for my kids. I am looking at a master's degree in Vocational Rehabilitation because I want to help others who are in situations such as the ones I had. I am looking for my passion for the work I do.

On Their Own Terms: Self-Directed Learners

The stories in "On Their Own Terms" capture the power and extent of personal learning in life. These people got bumped around and, in some cases slammed, by life. Drawing on their personal learning, they just had to find the path that worked for them, going over, under, around, and when necessary, through the obstacles before them.

Samuel Muraguri

Samuel Muraguri came to the United States in 2016 at the age of 34. He lives in western Washington and works as an auto-hauler for CarMax while running a growing small business out of his garage.

I was born in 1982 in a small town in Kenya. My parents had a very large family, five sons and one daughter. So, there was no silver spoon in my mouth from the start. It was a daily struggle for my parents with all the kids. When I graduated from high school in 2002, I moved to Nairobi and enrolled in an accounting program at a college there, the Vision Institute of Professionals. But that didn't work, and I had to drop out due to financial constraints.

So, I started out on my career path and went to work at a computer repair shop. Quite quickly, I learned how to fix computers, broken laptops, and broken screens, that kind of stuff. Within a year, I started my own business doing the same things. Eventually, we started reselling computers and assembling computers to be sold new.

Over the next 12 years, I came to realize that I needed something more. I realized that I was doing the same thing year in and year out but always hoping for a different result. Something had to change if I was going to turn my life around. We have a saying back home that says: If the mountain cannot come to you, then you have to go to the mountain. There are more people in Kenya who don't have jobs than people who do have jobs. And you might have the right idea and a good product, but the resources aren't there to support your success. I was building computers, but the customers didn't have the capacity to buy them. And the companies that could source stuff from China could beat you on price. So, I couldn't grow the company. And you know the old saying, "If you are working for your money, instead of having your money work for you, you are in the wrong place."

On top of all that, I didn't have a degree, and that was a killer in Kenya. So, I decided to come to America in 2016. My mother had come to the United States in 2010 in order to make more money so she could support the family back home. In 2016, I decided to do the same. I dropped everything, got a green card, and came to the US.

I had never been outside of Kenya. I had never even been on a plane. So, the whole travel thing was pretty amazing and very exciting! I flew from Kenya to Dubai to Seattle. The day I got off the plane in Seattle, it was cold and rainy, typical Seattle weather. But I had never been happier. It was February 2016.

I lived with Mom for about six months just to get acclimated and learn the community a little bit. Then I started my job search. I was a little worried because here I was with a Kenyan high school diploma looking for work in the United States. I felt a little high and dry in the beginning. But quite quickly, I saw an Amazon ad for warehouse workers, and I knew about Amazon. They were not asking for college degrees, and I got hired in June.

At first, I was packing packages. It was fun, and the pace was intense. Every night that we went in, there was a goal, and we had to meet that goal. I had always worked that way. I liked to set goals and hit them. So, it was fine. Then they moved me. At Amazon, they are always training you for different positions. In the new position, I was out of the mass production side of things and solving problems, like a special order that needed special treatment. Or a production line snafu that needed attention. I was getting paid to solve problems, and I liked that a lot better.

Amazon was very committed to educating its workers. They had a program called Career Choice where they paid 95% of the tuition, and you paid 5%. After working there for a year, I qualified for it. They had all these videos that told you the benefits of getting the training you wanted. So, I enrolled in order to get a better job. I never could have paid for it myself. And they even gave me a day shift schedule to accommodate my schooling. Very nice.

I passed the courses and got my Commercial Driver's License (CDL). I wanted to keep working but get out of doors and see the countryside, so the license was perfect. After I got the license, I left Amazon in 2017 when I got a job with the biggest used car reseller in the country, CarMax.

It was the outside work that I wanted, but it also came with a substantial raise. But the CDL was the key to getting the job. On top of that, I had references from former managers at Amazon. I had worked hard, met my goals, and ultimately worked without supervision. They supported me strongly.

As for Amazon and Career Choice, they encourage you to take the career path you desire. They really encouraged me to move up the ladder, even if that meant leaving. Their career choice program is intended to reward people who have met their goals, who respected others at work, and who showed them that they had the capacity to go farther. I was really surprised because they were explicit about helping me get the skills and then move if that was the best thing to do.

I was an auto transporter for CarMax. They trained me on how to load and unload the cars, and I already knew about time management and how to work solo. Also, working at Amazon, I was in a very diverse environment, and I learned a lot from my fellow workers. Everyone knows something that you do not. So, I learned a lot from all these different people. I also improved my language skills.

With the new job and the increased pay, I began to realize my dreams. In August 2018, I was able to buy my house. I believed in myself, and others did as well.

Getting a better-paying job also allowed me to send money home from time to time. I was helping my brothers and sister and their kids as they grew up and went to school. One of my brothers has finished University, the others have high school diplomas.

Looking back, the Career Choice program was the key to everything. It allowed me to change direction and improve myself. I feel very loyal to Amazon for that opportunity. Having just a high school diploma can be challenging if you are looking for a job that pays well. I took the direction that the new skill and license gave me. I credit Amazon with the direction I have developed.

In 2020, my new direction took another turn, and I started a new business at home in my garage. I said to myself, "If they could start Amazon in a garage, I can start my dream business in a garage." It is a coffee-roasting business, already fully licensed and inspected. Its name is Upendo Coffee (Upendo means "love" in Kenya). In Kenya, we drink a lot of tea. But here, people love their coffee. So, I wanted to aim at that market.

But I had an added dimension in mind for Upendo Coffee. We grow coffee in Kenya, but it has always been hard because there isn't enough market. So, I thought, why not create a direct link with the Kenyan growers and get them a better price and get their coffee to market in America? I identified the growers by asking my brother to talk to the coffee societies back home. He asked them what importers they were working with, and we identified one right here in Seattle. So, I will work through this importer until I have enough volume to go it alone.

I have a good business plan. One of the many things I learned at Amazon was the fulfillment process. On a day-to-day basis, I learned how it worked from A to Z. When the time came, I took all the information I had collected and put my plan together. It included selling through Amazon, and I am doing that now. I am a seller at Amazon, using their platform. I keep my coffee in their warehouses. I also sell through my own website UpendoCoffee.com, and I do local deliveries to anyone who lives within 10 miles, a few local stores, and the local farmer's market.

Both my girlfriend and I are still working other jobs. My girlfriend works in a hospital, and I still work at CarMax. We have different schedules, and that allows us to get all three jobs done: mine, hers, and Upendo.

I also learned automation at Amazon. If you automate, it makes everything easy. From the roasting all the way through to packaging, everything is automated.

I figured out the systems and, having worked with computers, I just did the research. I was self-taught – equipment, packaging, processes, printing, everything. I wanted the same result every time, so the roasting being automated was critical. It also made time management and higher productivity possible.

I am working towards one job, the coffee roasting business with an importing arm. Ultimately, I want to work with the Kenyan coffee growers and give them the love and the break that they need. Sometimes they don't get a fair price. I want to create a better price for them, maybe bring them here, let them see the process, and take that information home. That would be another way of saying "thank you."

Amazon's investment in me paid off in many ways. When I chose my own business, in yet another direction from driving, I wanted to do business with Amazon. So, what goes around comes around the full cycle.

If you had told me five years ago that all this was going to happen, I would have said you were crazy. I could not have anticipated the turnaround at Amazon due to Career Choice. And then the path opened up in front of me. Working at CarMax, my financial situation improved, and then I could think about another venture. I had the resources to think about a business of my own. I am self-taught all the way. My life experience has been my college.

Now I want to grow the business so I can give back love to the farmers and get them a fair price. They don't have a direct market, and I will believe in them the way others believed in me. One of the lessons I have learned is that everything is possible, and all it takes is a person to believe in you the way they did in me with the CDL.

Mother is so happy; she loves the coffee!

Chris Wilson

Chris Wilson is an artist, social entrepreneur, and philanthropist.

When I was younger, my mom and grandmom thought there was something wrong with me. I wasn't into sports, and I was interested in things like chess camp and playing the cello as a young teen. But all my friends teased me, and I finally stopped so that they would accept me.

I was not that great in school. And there was a lot of violence in the community, so I stayed indoors, and I read a lot. You know, stuff like *Man's Service for Meaning* by Frankel; *Made to Stick* by Dan and Chip Heath; *Thirty-Three Strategies for War; Malcolm X,* and Leil Lowndes's books on self-help.

Then, one day my mom's ex-boyfriend attacked us. He attacked me and hit me with a gun so hard that I was knocked out. When I came to, he was raping her. He tried to kill her right in front of me. My mom was never the same. But this guy was a cop, so he was lightly treated. After he got out of jail, he started stalking us. As a result, I started carrying a gun. There were guns everywhere. Because of the assault and the trauma and the pain (I was 14-15), things went to hell.

I remember getting nothing in school, drifting through life. At some point, my brother and cousin were shot, and my cousin died. Then the same people came after me one night, and I killed one of them. I was 17. When I was arrested, they charged me as an adult, and I was sent to jail for life as an 18-year-old. Then my brother and my dad were killed. Things were at rock bottom.

Around this time, my granddad was on his death bed, and he reached out and wanted to talk. He told me that I had to promise to do something good and to return to my cello/chess game mentality. At that point, I had no idea how to do that and even less inclination. I weighed 118, I was very depressed, and I was surrounded by older people in jail who said, "Relax, you're going to be here for a while."

Finally, I said to myself, "Okay, if this is my world, I'm going to start here."

The first thing I wanted was a high school diploma. Being that I was in prison, I had to figure out how to do that. So, I started trading cigarettes and stuff for tutoring in Algebra and other subjects. A guy named Steven became my mentor. Every time I got something wrong or did a function slower than the previous time, he made me drink a cup of water or do 25 pushups. So, I was learning, but I was also well-hydrated and in great shape. (Smiles.)

I graduated high school in two and a half months. The school was co-ed, and of course, some of the guys, including the staff, were interested in the girls. I agreed to guard the door and warn them if someone was approaching when they were fooling around. In return, I got access to the shop however I could pull it off. I also traded cigarettes to get into the shop and learn everything there—carpentry, sheet metal, plumbing, woodworking. I finished everything in 13 months. After every day, I cleaned the shop. The shop director loved me. I graduated from the vocational shop at 23.

Then, I met Tooky, another inmate, he was a little older, and he became a mentor to me. He got me to open up and get some therapy. The therapist wanted me to mentor others. I fought it, but he said, "Look, you are doing great and staying out of trouble. Maybe you can help some of the others."

About that time, I met another guy named Stephen. He was amazing and very interesting. Like, he was learning to code without a computer, just reading stuff and working on a pad. He told me he was going to get out, start a company and get rich. I laughed at how crazy that was. But he said, "Look around. They have taken everything, but we can't let them take our minds."

We ordered *Inc.* and the *Wall Street Journal*. His parents gave me a monthly Amazon book account. And we would read articles and books about the outside world. And we would argue and pretend to create and build companies. We are still connected, like every day. He started a software company, and it is growing. He started as an artist and is responsible for me becoming an artist—we are truly soul brothers. And we have always kept learning from each other and together.

At one point, they wanted us to put art around the prison. We got paid double. They wanted murals. I prepped, and he painted. At this point, I also started learning languages. Italian was first. They were starting a college program, and I got in. I thought I was way over my head. How do you write an essay? That kind of stuff. I was struggling, and I worked overtime: stayed after class, went to the computer center. The teacher was really hard on me, didn't bend the rules at all. But she helped, and I gradually improved.

Then I got into study groups. I read about a study on people who are learning second languages. I was studying Italian, and I wanted to include Spanish as well. To support this effort, I wanted to create a foreign language study group. I wrote the people doing the study who, after checking me out, took me and my language group on as part of their study.

Over time, I learned how I learned best. And I learned how to teach stuff to others in the prison. I started enjoying learning. I was eating better and exercising. Things like that.

My professors took an interest in me and Stephen and sent us books. We started a book club and stayed with it throughout. I studied business, real estate, Mandarin, other stuff. We wanted to start a business inside the prison to finance stuff for the general population. We asked for double pay, and they agreed. They got us two digital cameras, and we were off. We started with 6K in the bank, doubled the first year, and we were up to 20K the second year. To succeed, we had to learn the books, marketing, everything.

By this time, I had been there for 10 years. I asked for early release for the 10th time. I had done everything at the prison and not gotten in any trouble. They asked me to describe what I felt, and I told them about my mother's rape, my friends' murders, and that I had finished high school. The judge told me I had to excel and set an example. They reduced my sentence and agreed to send me to a halfway house. But folks on the inside were worried that I would screw up, so they added some years. So, even with the "early release," I had to wait four more years. During that time, I did a lot more learning, including A+ certification and Mandarin, as well as a lot more therapy and self-knowledge.

I finally got out and went to the University of Baltimore. I was a straight-A student. But, once again, my past caught up with me. One day my mother called me and yelled at me to be "good." I told her to relax, and we argued. A very unpleasant conversation. She hung up and committed suicide. I went into a deep depression, and my halfway house counselor sent me back to prison. Ultimately, they sent me to another prison. Fairly quickly, I got a release hearing, and they granted me parole again. But I didn't get out until two months later.

Once again, I had nothing. I was starting all over again. I was going to apply for food stamps and get a job. I bought a lawnmower and a $10 phone and started a lawn mowing business. And my professors were ready to take me back. Then I got a job at the University. So, I bought a bike and went. I was Director of Workforce Development. I loved it and worked very hard.

I got into a B.A. business program. It was very strict. We presented at every class. There was a dress code, and you had to check all electronics at the door. You had to come up with a business idea and prove you could create profit with it to graduate. One day the professor said, "Get up, close your book, and go find proof of concept. Think about your idea as a virus and go figure out how to spread it."

My first idea was furniture restoration which I had learned in prison. There was a hotel near the university that looked as if it needed restoration. Cal Ripken frequented it quite a bit as a customer, and he spent a lot of time at the lounge. And I thought that was cool. So, long story short, I got a contract to do their hotel. I went to a bank and got some cash. Went back to class with the contract and the money—laid them out, and my professor started crying. That beginning turned into doing big hotels, and it was a very successful business.

But it was frustrating because part of my vision was to improve the community. And there were many people in the community who I couldn't employ because of the scale of my business. So, I started another company, construction, and I was able to hire 23 additional people. As these successes were just beginning, I had anxiety because I had spent half my life in jail. Some of my professors and staff wanted me to deny it, to sweep it under the rug. But, after I finally came clean about the whole thing, many others came up and hugged me. They gave me more business because I had come clean.

I was living near a lot of artists. Jeffrey Kent, a friend who was an artist, gave me lessons. I was winning competitions and making money. Then an old dream resurfaced. I decided to write a book. I had determined to do this when I was 19 and in jail. But I didn't get to it for 20 years. But never a dull moment. I had to go to court to win permission to do the book. The Son of Sam statute says that a person cannot profit off their crime. I wasn't writing about my crime. I was writing about my life and what I had learned.

The book, *The Master Plan: My Journey from Life in Prison to a Life of Purpose*, captivated people, and they reached out to me. Then, I was the Executive Producer for a movie, "The Box." And although that wasn't part of my initial intention, I wanted to tell the story that you can go do good stuff no matter what. I wanted to share that story and make it happen for other people. That was life-changing and getting an advance and a movie deal really turned me around. My life became a dream. I began to paint and, as I painted, I forgot about my troubles.

Now two years later, I am selling paintings and giving books away. And I started the Chris Wilson Foundation. We fund artists. I am funding a prison art program and financial literacy programs. I want people to learn how to save and be wise with money; I want to support small lines of credit for local organizations that want to help the community that banks won't touch.

In 2015, when Freddie Gray was killed, I got more involved. Dove in, went to hearings on capitol hill, received an award from President Obama. My publisher held back money on the basis that he couldn't profit from a crime. But we won that one as well, though it hurt me financially.

Now I've been to 24 countries. I got sick with COVID in January and almost passed. Nobody knew what it was. Lots of my friends got it, including my doc. In the lockdown, I just kept painting and selling and doing seminars.

It has been essential to my success to leverage my network to succeed, to build, to learn. It started with Steve and Tooky in prison. A mutual thing.

When I am sitting with people for the first time, they tend to assume they are smarter than me. But I am smarter than they think. I learned a lot over the years. A lot of this was outside school—either experience, classes, or on my own. For example, Mandarin was a great thing to learn in prison. Thousands of years, tradition, culture. And I am still studying it.

More generally, I would say that everyone, no matter where they come from, should have a master plan, a strategy, and an end game. It gives you purpose. I am an artist more than anything else now. People buy it and that's good.

Rahim Fazal

Rahim Fazal is a serial entrepreneur and founder of SV Academy.

My parents were immigrants from East Africa in the '70s. They fled Idi Amin's dictatorship and moved to Canada, British Columbia, in 1981. I was born in 1982 and grew up there. I ultimately moved to the US in 2006.

It was a tough childhood economically. My dad was trained as a pharmacist, but the Canadian licensing rules didn't recognize his credential because it was from overseas, so he had to work as a parking lot attendant. My mom had her diploma in microbiology, but that was not recognized either. So, she stayed home to raise my sister and me. Ultimately, she became a pre-school teacher. So, they sort of went from the top to the bottom as a consequence of immigrating.

We lived in government housing until I was 12. I was a good student and really loved elementary school. The elementary school experience, through seventh grade, was more personal and intimate. For example, I had the same teacher and students in every class. I knew a lot of the same people. And the environment was quite flexible. I loved technology and games, and when I was building games at school, it was as if I was playing. By the time I was eight, I was also reading magazines and books, sort of self-teaching. My parents were very supportive. Even though we didn't have much money, they gave me a lot of time, and there was a lot of structured play.

Then, along came high school. At the most basic level, like Maslow's hierarchy of needs, I felt that I needed to contribute to the family, so I got a part-time job. Frankly, that sort of complicated things and took me off task when it came to school. But there were other problems as well. I was attending a private Catholic school, and my parents paid the tuition even though they didn't have much money. We thought it would be an improvement, but it turned out we were wrong. It was almost the exact opposite of my earlier experiences. For example, all the learning was highly structured. And they publicly posted honors grades which fostered grade competition. It really changed things for me because I am a very competitive guy. In retrospect, I saw that I started working for the grade, not the joy of learning. And that was not a good thing.

In addition to that, there was a lot of systemic racism at that school as well. For starters, I was a Muslim in a Catholic school. And coupled with that, there was much less diversity than the public school I had attended. I was singled out quite a bit, and, as a result, I began acting out and got in trouble. I really wanted to get out of there.

After two years, I left and went to the public high school for grades 10-12. At the high school, I applied to and was admitted to the International Baccalaureate program, thinking that would be interesting. But as it turned out, I really didn't like the overall experience at the public high school that much either.

As I can recognize now, I didn't see the value of the outcome. Why was I doing this? I couldn't see the connection between what I was being asked to do and any long-term value. The socialization was good. There were a lot of parties and stuff like that. But there were 3000 students there. It was impersonal and, overall, the classes sucked. It just wasn't for me; a cookie-cutter, factory-style approach. All you had to do was read the text, memorize the material, and regurgitate it. So, I did well because I had a good memory. But the actual learning that I hungered for, learning for change and transformation, just wasn't there.

In 11th grade, I was isolated from the main student body, studying only with my International baccalaureate peers. I was lonely, bored, and frustrated. Not coincidentally, that was the year that I started building my first company with my friend Hussein. Now, building the company was really exciting. So, I dropped out of the IB program at the end of the year to give myself more time to work on the company. And, by the end of 12th grade, we had sold the company.

But finishing the 11th grade was tough. I was in the full IB program, I had a job after school, and Hussein and I were building this company on the side. I'd go to work after school at 4 p.m. and work till 10. Then I'd go home and to bed and be up by 6:30 the next morning. I had to take the bus and a train to school. So, overall, the schedule was really intense.

Also, working got me down. It was a fast-food place, and there was no bigger picture, nothing to aspire to there. I'm looking at people who have worked there for 20 years, and they are not going anywhere. That's not what I wanted. What's the point of it all? Like high school, there was no big picture, and I was sure there was something bigger out there. And to be honest, on a personal level, I didn't like people telling me what to do, and I was probably goofing off a little. Finally, they let me go, and that was ok with me. I missed the money and didn't like getting fired. But there was no lasting damage. (He laughs.) And it gave me more time and incentive to develop the company because my evenings were free.

The company just came along out of the blue. Hussein and I had been trying to find something to do. We investigated Silicon Valley and read about entrepreneurs. What inspired us was reading magazines about these people who were not much older than us who were doing cool things. We decided that we could do that too. So as a hobby, we began to build a web-hosting business. You don't know what you don't know. And we didn't know how to get access to capital or build a company. Instead, we connected with the creative experience. That was what drove us. We played to our strengths out of necessity.

Growing the business while going to school was the hardest part. But I learned how to build web pages and do guerilla marketing online. I had the instinctive business savvy and knew what to build and how to market it. Hussein was the coder, the guy who set up the servers. We did it from scratch, and when we didn't know something, we learned from reading and talking to people who did know.

Looking back on it, the whole thing was pretty bizarre. I worked at home, but we both hid what we were doing from our parents. By the end of the senior year, we had 25K users, and a company reached out to us to partner. But it turned into "why don't we buy the whole thing." The selling sort of unfolded, almost effortlessly. We weren't pushing a particular solution. We just reacted to what was happening.

Two funny stories. First, we set up a phone number for user issues. It was my cell phone, and my girlfriend recorded the answering machine message and made it sound like a real professional operation. I got calls in school and repeatedly asked to be excused from class. And the calls were so frequent when I was at home that my parents decided that I was selling drugs. I assured them that was not the issue. And although they tried, they never knew what I was really doing until it was reported in the newspaper after the sale.

Also, we created a video call to begin the sales process. But I had an older white gentleman stand in for me because I thought the potential customers wouldn't take it well if they saw the two skinny, brown-skinned teenagers who were actually running it. So, we finally sold it for $1.5M. After paying the taxes, giving some to my parents, and having some fun, we started another business. But that one failed, and we lost the rest of the money.

So now I am 21. I have no degree and no money. I went to the community college, but it was a joke. I knew everything that I was studying. I had an instructor who really helped me out. She said that I was wasting my time and introduced me to the Dean of the Ivey Business School at Western University. I was admitted into the MBA program there with no associate or baccalaureate degree! Just leap-frogged to the MBA.

I took a straight course academically, and the program lasted two years. Although I did learn some new stuff, what I really got was the language and the frameworks that explained what I had learned experientially while building the business. In addition, I felt valued, and it was a great convergence experience.

On another front, I also learned about networks and how privileged people use them to get ahead. That's what I got for the tuition. That's what it bought. A framework for my knowledge and access to networks of privilege. It was my first experience with people who were born wealthy. And I was amazed to learn that many of them were following in their parents' footsteps; that they had always assumed they would go there after high school. And I was pretty naïve. For example, once I went to a pool party, and a guy showed up in Gucci shorts and loafers with no socks. I had never seen anything like that before. I was shocked.

After graduation, in 2006, I went to Silicon Valley. I began to network, and I interviewed at Google and eBay. They both turned me down, and the punchline was that they were very elitist. One woman told me, "I think you'd be better off starting with investment banking on Wall Street." All of a sudden, the message is that I should go straight. And that was exactly what I didn't want to do. I experienced a lot of elitism and racism as I tried to access the jobs I wanted. And even when I penetrated and got through the first round, the interviews were stacked against me.

Ultimately, I got an interview with a small firm in Palo Alto run by some Canadian ex-pats. They were small, they hadn't gone to fancy schools, and they loved my story because it was like theirs. They hired me, and I worked there. I got an idea for a piece of software for sales on Facebook. I developed it over the next five years while we built it to about $10M. Then we sold it to Oracle when I was 30.

I went to Oracle to work as part of the deal. So now I am shoulder to shoulder with McKinsey-trained people and Harvard/Stanford grads. Getting exposed to all their sales talent really opened my eyes. And I realized that sales were really what turned me on. It was great to finally understand that sales were at my core, a real turning point. Sales were a career path with a front door. What would happen if I could help a whole lot of people like me find that front door?

At Oracle, however, I am on the other side of the divide. I had made it. So, the question for me became, "What am I going to do next? I had met a guy, a senior person at Hewlett-Packard, named Joel. We talked about what came next. Joel had always done just what his parents wanted—McGill, Stanford Law, and HP. And he was unfulfilled at that level. He was saying, "I feel unfulfilled." And I was saying, "I need to work with someone who is a strong operator with compatible values while I am out selling." That was Joel. He was my next Hussein.

Meanwhile, while all of the story was playing out after I moved to America, I'd been telling my story on Tedx Talks, at the White House, at MIT, and at President Obama's Global Entrepreneurship Summit in Dubai. I really enjoyed doing this. It was heady stuff, and the audiences seemed to enjoy it as well. But there was one big nagging problem. I could tell my story, talk about my success and "what" I had done. But I couldn't describe how someone else could do it. I could not describe the "how" and that bugged me.

That was a very influential moment. Two strands of thought came together. First, I knew that I wanted to help people like me get into the business in spite of the obstacles. I wanted to start a school. Oracle is very large and very sales-oriented company. They hired a ton of people out of college, but they only focused on eight to ten very prestigious colleges. If you made the cut, then you were on the farm team. But if you didn't work out, you were gone. It was as wasteful as it was biased. The opportunity was not accessible to many people. It focused on the elite.

And second, I needed to focus on the "how" question and get an answer in order to start the type of school I had in mind. I was genuinely excited by the opportunity to help people like the younger me get the opportunity and learn the answer to the "how" question, how do you create successful salespeople, and how do they perform?

I saw the chance to combine the skills needed with actual employment opportunities and share that knowledge and opportunity across multiple settings. And that's where the SV Academy came from. The academy is a mindset and philosophy, but it is also a platform with lots of courses and information.

Here's how it works. It is similar to a school in that there is an admissions process. If you meet certain requirements, you gain access. It is cohort-based with monthly starts. Every cohort is either full-time for four weeks or part-time for 12 weeks. The focus is on sales. It is a rigorous experience, including skill-building with industry mentors on how to do the work before you are doing the work. It is modeled on what entry-level work in sales is actually like.

Then you get matched with employers, get a job, and go to work. The second layer comes over the next 12 months—coaching, up-skilling, a long tail to support and emphasize learning on the job. We stay with our learners throughout that year because the work experience lies at the core of the essential learning they have to do to be successful.

There was luck along the way, yes. And there were events and people who made a difference in my life. But now I get to give back. I am running a business that helps thousands of people like me bust the privilege system, get access to networks and communities that were previously inaccessible, and then sustain the change.

Michelle Daniels

Michelle Daniels is completing her Ph.D. program at NYU. A holder of multiple degrees and certificates, she is also a prolific author and advocate for change in the criminal justice system. She is President of the Board of Constructing Our Future, a non-profit created and led by previously incarcerated women to provide a home base and support for those who follow them.

I grew up in Indiana and went to IUPUI before I was incarcerated. After I got out, I enrolled in graduate school at NYU, and now I am back home because of COVID-19 and the fact that I can write my dissertation from anywhere. My topic is: How are people surviving incarceration? We know little of the psychic and social toll, and so I'm interested in those aspects and what people are doing to survive incarceration. What happens to the people who don't survive is also of great interest to me.

It's been an amazing journey. For starters, I was incarcerated in 1997 when I was 25 years old. And I served almost 21 years out of a 25-year term with four years off in earned credit time. As for life before incarceration, I was really interested in computers, and they were in my schools since around the seventh grade. Back then, I was going to be a systems analyst.

At first in prison, I was in a state of self-loathing, cleaning toilets, and content to do what I was doing. I had no desire to do anything more with myself. But a woman named Vanessa Williams was my counselor, and she wasn't having any of it. She came after me and told me to snap out of it. I had capability. I had worked at Eli Lilly and was head of my class in a magnet school. And Vanessa's whole thing was, "Michelle, you've got something. You must not sit in here and do nothing."

She helped me understand that I could learn and move on. She helped me move through my grief and take hold of things. So, I started learning everything I could. First, I learned the law and became a certified paralegal. The program taught you how to research the law and build a legal argument. I developed an actual petition to help the women petition the court for custody of their children. There was a temporary guardianship form they could use, but I wanted to make sure that the women could get their children back when they came home – the same with divorces and other personal legal matters.

I then learned building trades and maintenance. I wanted to challenge myself, and I learned that I could do these things that I had never done before. I helped people get their building trades certificates and prepare for journeyman training and licenses if they wanted to follow that path.

Copyright © by Michelle Daniel Jones. Reprinted by permission.

We were fortunate at this particular facility because there were two colleges involved—Martin University, a predominately African-American college, and Ball State. We worked all day and then went to school at night. I loved it and really dug in deep with those teachers who cared and went the extra mile with us. That extra work made all the difference. I started with Martin, and I had a few courses that transferred from IUPUI. But I ended up at Ball State when, out of nowhere, Martin was kicked out of the prison, which left me hanging with 96 credits. When I transferred, I lost 46 credits in the process. Worse than that, the state gave you only eight semesters to complete a bachelor's, and I had already used most of those. Bottom line, at Ball State, I got to my senior year and was out of semesters. I discussed it with one of my professors, and the money was found to allow me to finish my coursework.

I did not know at the time that the scholarship came from him personally. Long after I got my degree, he told me he did it and helped get the additional funds from some Franciscan monks in Muncie, Indiana. Very, very amazing that he took the time to find the resources. I was about to lose everything, and he came through for me. I graduated summa cum laude, doing some awesome stuff, including writing my business and marketing plan for the non-profit I was planning.

Getting the B.A. from Ball State also allowed me to attend seminary while still in prison. Luckily, I was able to participate in the Education for Ministry program run by St. John's Episcopal Church, where they paid for four years of training via the Sewanee Theological Seminary. The folks from St. John's came in weekly to do the teaching. When that was done, I had paralegal, A.D., B.A., and Seminary. After that, I finished the building trades program and became a production assistant in 2011.

When Ball State left, Oakland City University, a small private university in Oakland, Indiana, came in. I went to work for them, doing tutoring first as a volunteer and then employed as a clerk. Also, working as a volunteer, I helped start the "One Net One Life" Mosquito Net Project. They were looking at the connection between entrepreneurship and service. The idea was to create mosquito nets. One of my colleagues was asked to come up with a prototype net. And the class ended up doing a ton of research. They met a woman who had been a world traveler. She had a new idea for a dramatically different prototype. It was rectangular as opposed to cone-shaped, sealing the person inside the bed or mat. It was useable in multiple settings and didn't need any metal supports. It was considered the Cadillac of nets by all who used them.

Sherrell Russel and I worked with the University to get the resources and funds to begin production. Within weeks, we began to manufacture nets and shortly thereafter send them to Africa. The program is now a part of the Community Outreach program of the facility. Our orientation was that we would give the nets away in return for the purchase of supplies. We also did fundraisers with the women and raised money to make the program go. So, I was doing that for four to five years completely as a volunteer.

Then, the money to subsidize Oakland City U was cut out of the state budget in 2012. I will never forget it. I was called early one morning, and the program coordinator told me that they would be leaving at the end of the year. OCU had made the prison an actual university satellite site, amazingly, and now they were defunded. They called in all of the students and told them. It was devastating.

But then Dr. Kelsey Kaufman brought in her expertise and built a non-credit higher education program. She taught public policy, history, and other classes. She brought in volunteer and retired faculty to provide coursework to students. This was where "Constructing Our Future," of which I am Board President, was birthed. As part of the program, Kelsey came up with the idea that students would research the facility they were in. It started with undergrads paired with graduates. We were going to look into the history of the facility from the beginning. The course went over two semesters because the materials were right there, and there was so much of it. Ultimately, we founded the Indiana Women's Prison History Project, which is still ongoing. There is so much to this history that it has many angles of research. The questions were numerous. The history we were writing had never been captured before. The angle of our research changed how benevolent reformers in Indiana are viewed—why did the women try to burn the place down twice? Why was the treatment of incarcerated women little better with women leadership than men? In the process, we reclaimed the voices of women and girls incarcerated in Indiana institutions. We began to give academic presentations, beginning with the Indiana Historical Association and then on to the American History Association. Ultimately, we published in local and national publications.

As my departure from prison approached, Kelsey had a conversation with me about my future. I had decided that I wanted to fundamentally change how women and men are treated when they come into contact with the criminal justice system and prisons specifically including the ongoing dehumanization, poor living conditions, and all the rest. When I shared that with Kelsey, she suggested that I get a Ph.D. I was completely at a loss for words. No one I knew had ever gotten a Ph.D. Kelsey said those programs come with a stipend and no tuition. I had never heard of anything like that, and I didn't know anyone who had done it. I was in disbelief—both that she thought this was real and that it was something I could do.

One of the women who was teaching was a post-doctoral student. I told her what I was interested in – history, American studies—and asked her to look into opportunities. I had taken some graduate courses on genocide, debt and dispossession, race and sexuality, and the Vietnam War—so I knew I could do it. She brought me a ton of options, and I spent the weekends looking through them and coming up with my top five. But Kelsey laughed them down. She asked, "Why didn't you choose some of the ones I did?" She thought I was aiming too low. Then, she went to her national conference (The American Studies Association) with my CV in hand and mentioned me to different faculty members there. And then, we created a master list, and I ended up applying to nine schools.

I had to work on describing my own narrative, including my criminal history so that I didn't get blowback later on. And that was traumatizing because it re-triggered a bunch of things. Still, I got into five schools and two departments at another school. Some asked for permission to do a background check, saying it was a formality because they knew I was applying while incarcerated. It was actually an excuse to reject me. Ultimately, one rescinded their award letter, and I pulled out from another before they could rescind it.

I chose the school with the most support, guaranteed housing, and a good stipend. They worked really hard to get me additional housing in the future years because they knew that formerly incarcerated people are cosmically discriminated against in housing. That was the decision-maker for me. I was very anxious about the whole idea of having safe housing, and anything that could be resolved and decided made a big difference emotionally. And I wanted to take care of myself. This attitude came from being deeply disappointed in the important people in my life in the early days before incarceration, where I learned how to take care of myself as a matter of necessity.

So here I am, three years later. There is a calling in my life. Formerly incarcerated people are subjected to all sorts of discrimination and barriers that affect our right to move forward. We are treated as scarred. I am driven by this fight to provide pathways for healing and starting lives over. And I support us doing that.

I am willing to work with everyone toward real, meaningful change, but I want more than an ally. I want advocates and co-conspirators, like my professor, people who are willing to work with us to change how people who were incarcerated are thought of; people who have the ability to support our leadership, allowing our knowledge and lived experience of incarceration to inform decisions.

In order to get to my calling, I had to deal with my failures and shortcomings. I had to deal with my "stuff," personally and socially. This is a continuing process. But now, I am positioned to go and do the work I was called to do. I can see my path, and I want to be a good steward of that path. That path is built on my past, but it is aimed at changing realities in the future. A lot of people helped me and are helping me today, and that is essential. I can't do this alone, but I also had to learn to help myself, to like myself, to trust myself. When I do something myself, I learn to stand on sure footing. If I do the part I am called to do, then I can work with others as well. But if I don't help myself, I won't be able to help others.

Section 3:
Bridges to the Future

People and Programs

"Important People and Programs" describes how learners benefitted tremendously from people they met along the way; people who advised and advocated for them. Much is made of mentoring and support. But for advice to be truly helpful, it should be connected to a pathway towards opportunity. And the impact of these "important people" in learners' lives and the programs that they connected the learners to in many cases cannot be overestimated.

Katie Reigelsperger

Katie is 32, the mother of her two sons, Joshua and Daniel, and the Owner and Instructor for KLR Pharmacy Technician Training School, teaching full time primarily for The Excel Center, sponsored by GoodWill.

I grew up in Indiana, moving from one town or city to the next. For as long as I can remember, my parents were drug addicts and alcoholics. My mother lived in a different state and was consumed with her alcoholism. As a result, I spent only a handful of days with her during my childhood. My father, apparently the more "put together" of the two, took on the role of taking care of my sister and me.

I lived with my father, but I wasn't any safer with him than I would have been with my mom. He was married four times in 12 years. Each of these women was a new "mother" for me, for which I was told I should be thankful. Each one went down his dark, destructive path with him, and each one was more dangerous and cruel than the one that came before. He drank away his problems and swallowed pills to ease his worries while my sister and I showed up to school hungry and with bruises down our backs and legs. He turned a blind eye while we were made to eat food we didn't like and then made us eat the throw up off the ground that followed that. My father was in continuous trouble with the law; he spent several months on house arrest, years on probation, and was in and out of jail. He was a habitual offender and landed himself in prison for a year when I was ten and in the fifth grade.

I switched schools five times during my fifth-grade year and eventually ended up with a foster family for the last portion of that year. My father promised a fresh start for all of us when he was released and was sure that fresh start was in Indianapolis, a couple hours away from where I was currently living. But as always, his inner demons got the best of him, and that night, with no place to live and no vehicle or driver's license, he checked us into a hotel and drank himself into a stupor. And so, the cycle continued on. In sixth grade, I switched schools only three times, and by the end of eighth grade, I'd made some friends and was feeling a bit more settled.

But after years of bad examples and in a very impressionable time of my life, I was lost and confused. I ended up pregnant at thirteen years old, giving birth to my first child just after finishing my eighth-grade year.

Though I had worked at Burger King throughout my pregnancy to save up for items I would need when the baby arrived, I wasn't sure how I was going to work, go to school, and pay for childcare as well as take care of a baby. According to my father, this was a situation I had gotten myself into, and I needed to figure it out on my own. His only source of "assistance" was to withdraw me from school with promises to the staff that I would be homeschooled, not that he ever had any intentions of doing so.

It was far from an ideal situation, but by this time in my life, I had developed some grit. I made flyers and hung them up at the local libraries and grocery stores and acquired a few children to babysit each day to help make ends meet. I was too young to live on my own, and so my father told me that I would be required to pay a portion of the rent and a monthly fee to help with the electricity if I wanted to place my son's food in the refrigerator.

From a young age, I knew I didn't want a life similar to the one I was living. I had goals and dreams. I loved school, and I spent every moment that I could reading and writing. At a very young age, I wanted to be a teacher, and as I grew older, I had dreams of going to Harvard, majoring in law and minoring in journalism. My experiences with the law, specifically the disheartening ones, made me want to fight for children in situations like mine, where no one seemed to be even listening, must less speaking up for me. I was a good debater and arguer and could imagine myself as an attorney.

I was also interested in journalism; I have always loved reading; it's an act that allows you to be taken away and imagine anything is possible regardless of where you are in your life. Writing is a hobby, a stress-reliever, and a coping mechanism for me. It allows me to put onto paper the bad things that have happened and decipher those situations for myself in my own time, and at the same time, it allows me to plan out and decide what and who I want to become. I've taken these things with me throughout the years, and to this day, I spend a significant amount of time both reading and journaling.

When I was almost 16, I moved in with the father of my child, who was 13 years older than me; a man who took advantage of my young age and who should have known better. But, at the very least, I was away from my father, and I had no intention of ever returning to his home. I spent two years there and gradually realized more and more that not only was I not happy, but that my own thought processes were much different from this man. To me, this had been a little girl crush, not love, and I was growing up and was ready to move on.

So, my journey of finding who I was and who I wanted to be began. The first step in this process for me was to study for my GED; checking out books from the local library. Neither of my parents had finished high school, and though I knew that I couldn't go to a traditional high school while raising my son, I could at least earn the equivalent of a high school diploma. I took and passed the GED exam months after my 16th birthday. The second step was to leave the relationship I was in—an unhealthy relationship with a man whose choices changed my life forever. However, choices I can never regret because they brought me my son.

I met Daniel's father when I was 18, and I gave birth to my second son the day before my 19th birthday. But again, I was young, and our relationship was toxic.

I moved out and rented a small trailer; though ultimately, most of my life I'd felt alone, this was the first time I was living on my own with a five-year-old and a newborn baby. Although I had earned my GED years prior, and it was an accomplishment that I could be proud of, it didn't aid me in finding a job that would pay enough to make ends meet, that provided health insurance I could afford, or that rewarded me with any sort of paid time off. I worked as the Lead Teacher for two-year-olds at KinderCare, a childcare facility, but I couldn't afford the cost of keeping my children in care while I worked, so I eventually ended up working at the local Marsh Supermarket and waitressing part-time at a restaurant near me.

The kids and I lived in that trailer for a few years, struggling to make ends meet, and I continued to find myself with not enough time to help my son with his homework and keep up with day-to-day tasks. Daniel's father and I decided to give our relationship another shot, and we moved in with him, which allowed me to stay home with the kids and focus on them for the next couple of years while babysitting to bring in a small income. In 2012, my mother died of cancer caused by smoking and drinking.

Fast forward a couple of years, my story really took a turn. While waiting for my kids to finish a martial arts lesson in 2013, I overheard a conversation about the Excel Center—a high school for adults. I quickly asked questions of my own and was enrolled the next day. Joshua was 10 and in the fifth grade, and it was important that he see me receive a high school education and know that I believed in its importance.

The Excel Center is supported by Goodwill. It is an optional high school for adults of all kinds—old, young, pregnant, near-finishers, and people like me. It is completely free, with all expenses covered and childcare provided at no additional cost. It is a program that allows you to work at your own pace to reach your goals, but I knew that this was something I needed to do now.

Within my first month of classes, we found my father dead in his home from a drug overdose. It was a heart-wrenching, bittersweet, and soul-searching time for me. And this experience at the Excel Center was the next step in my journey to finding myself and becoming who I wanted to be and making sure I gave my children a childhood they didn't have to overcome. I was 25 years old with not a day of high school experience. I had zero credits, but I had an infinite amount of determination. In eight months, I earned 42 credits and two certifications; the first in early childhood, which was simple due to my experience at KinderCare years prior, and the second was a Pharmacy Technician Certification.

My experience at Kindercare was all I needed for the early childhood certificate. I didn't have to look at a book. At Kindercare, I had drawn on my experience as a mom. I watched others at work and worked intently with the children. Pretty quickly, I had been moved up to lead teacher. When they offered the course at the Excel Center,

I took it simply as a backup plan. But when I took the test, it was completely based on concepts I had already done at Kindercare—like getting down on the same level as the child you are speaking with.

This was a turning point for me. Daniel's father proposed to me, and we got married the same week that I graduated. And on the day of my graduation both of my children sat in the front row looking on with pride as their mother received her high school diploma with honors and a 3.8 GPA. A week after graduation, I received a job offer from CVS and worked up to being the lead technician and inventory specialist in the pharmacy in a pretty short period of time. At the same time, I was applying to hospitals where I could receive more training and experience. I received an offer from a local hospital, Riverview Health, and started there on my 26th birthday as an in-patient pharmacy technician, again with no experience. My starting wage was $13.50 per hour, significantly more than I had ever earned before. Additionally, for the first time, I was able to provide my children and myself with health insurance, and I had paid time off in addition to other benefits.

A year and a half later, in 2016, I had learned all the basics—chemo, IV, med history—and I was promoted to pharmacy technician supervisor. At the same time, I was a member of the county hazmat team and learning a different set of skills there. As the supervisor, I was in charge of the ongoing training, scheduling, and oversight of approximately 30 technicians, and it was a truly rewarding time, full of learning and growth. Ronald Reagan once said, "The greatest leader is not necessarily the one who does the greatest things; he is the one that gets the people to do the greatest things." The opportunity to lead a group to their potential and bring a team together was a joy for me.

It seemed that my life was finally falling together on a path I'd worked so hard to get to. But my relationship with Daniel's father, the love of my life and my best friend, was deteriorating, and I was at a point in my life where I needed to see that I could do things on my own. So, in 2018, I filed for divorce and moved into an apartment with the kids. The kids were growing up, and I had a career. I had to make this work. It was a life-changing move. But, even with the money I was making, it was almost impossible financially, emotionally, and physically. I was working full-time at the hospital with a demanding job, taking a couple of college courses, and working three to four nights a week as a waitress. Daniel was 10 and Joshua was almost 15 and, first and foremost, I needed to be present as their mother.

In September of 2019, while we were driving to Georgia for a family camping trip (from which I had no idea how we were even going to get home financially), I got a call from the Excel Center, asking me if I'd be willing to teach a Pharmacy Technician Certification course for them. I knew I wasn't a teacher, and I had no experience as such, but I did have the certification as a pharmacy technician, and I was in charge of teaching these training skills and basics to my team at the hospital each day; so, I decided to give it a try.

When I gave birth to Joshua at 13, I felt totally alone. And throughout the years, I continued to feel like I would never get out of the situation I was in. I wished many times that I could speak with someone who had endured my struggles and could help guide me. So many of the students I've met and worked with in the last year and a half have experiences just like mine. They are people who were "given a bad hand of cards" and who need a second chance, having been denied the first chance by no decision of their own. By sharing my story with these incredible students, they could identify their lives with mine, and I've been given the opportunity to use my past experiences to help mentor and guide others; assuring them that they are not a product of their childhoods and that they do not have to be what they came from. Helping them and being there for them in this way has been one of the greatest honors of my life.

The students who take this course have a plan laid out for them; The Excel Center walks them through each step of the licensing process and has programs that will aid them in finding employment. So not only are they graduating with a high school diploma, they have a certification and a license to practice, which sets them apart from other applicants, making them employable.

The class has continued to grow and succeed, and in October of 2020, I resigned from my position at the hospital to teach this course full time. Currently, the goal is to expand the course to make it available to students in other states, which would not be possible without the support and encouragement of Goodwill and The Excel Center.

The events of my childhood, the ones that I did not choose, have shaped me as a person, and I will never forget them. But I learned early on to forgive others, not because they deserve it, but because I deserve peace. Throughout my journey, I've carried forward many other lessons. I learned that the only person I can really count on is myself, that I have to be my own biggest fan. I learned to question who I trust by being hurt and let down so many times by those who should have loved me most but didn't. These "lessons of life" have turned me into a leader who refuses to quit, someone who always works hard and knows that anything worth having is worth working hard for. I'm naturally more optimistic because I realize how hard things can really be. I take ownership of my own decisions and actions, and I realize that every one of them has consequences, whether good or bad. In every kind of relationship that I have, I strive to be honest, kind, loyal, and reliable. I fully believe that I've taken more learning, more lessons, and more good out of the bad that was handed to me because the bad taught me to structure the way I looked at my life and reach for more.

Despite many others telling me that, "It can't be done. A baby can't raise a baby, and he will turn out just like you, and unfortunately, you are destined to end up like your parents." I'm 32 and Joshua is 17. We grew up together. My life goal has been to provide my children with a childhood that they do not need to recover from. I'm proud to say that a part of that prediction was right. Joshua went on to follow in my footsteps—he graduated high school early, with honors. He currently resides at Ball State University, where he is majoring in Business Administration. He is serving in the National Guard and has goals to train to become a pilot. Joshua has told me time and time again that watching me struggle and never give up has had a major impact on his life. His younger brother, Daniel, is 13, is in all advanced classes, and is thinking of joining the military as well in a few short years.

I believe that our character is defined by what we do when no one else is looking. Life lessons, those soft skills we speak of as employers, while teachable through experience, can't be taught in a classroom. And a person who has pushed through every obstacle to reach their goals will find a way to succeed despite the trials and tribulations thrown at them on the way. I haven't lived my life in the sequence of events that we've been made to believe is the only way, but I made it, nonetheless. Society would like us to believe that we are stuck when we missed the opportunity for education when it was available; and that it was our fault. But it wasn't. It was simply a person's life, and you are not defined by your past, but you can be prepared by it.

Calvin Duker

Calvin Duker is married and the father of three children. He holds a master's degree and manages human resource recruitment at nine charter schools for CSMI Educational Management in Chester, Pennsylvania.

My family moved to Cecilton, Maryland, when I was six or seven. That was a huge change for me because I had grown up on a farm with my mom and my aunt and uncle. My dad was never really in the picture. And here I was in a new town with new people and a totally different lifestyle. But there was some good news that came with the new surroundings.

Earlier in my childhood, when I was five, I was almost kidnapped. I had gone to the store with my aunt at the Kmart. I got separated from my aunt, and this lady came up to me and said she could take me back to her. But she took me out to the parking lot, and she was putting me into her car. I was terrified and crying. Just in the nick of time, a neighbor came into the parking lot and saved me. She intervened and asked me if I was ok. I said, "No." She took me away from the lady, and we went and found my aunt in the store. I was completely undone by this, shattered and terrified.

The trauma of that episode affected my speech. I didn't talk, and I had therapy of one kind or another for several years. I got held back in kindergarten because I wasn't speaking. But after we moved, I did better. I adjusted to the change in living, and my speech was improving. But my reading still wasn't so hot. In fact, I was in Special Education all the way to middle school for reading, math, and writing. And to put it mildly, I was an average student all the way through.

My fifth-grade year teacher told my mom that I wasn't college material and to think about trade school. But I ended up going to the Cecilton Elementary School/Bohemian Manor High School in Chesapeake. We didn't want to get pushed off the track. Mom wanted me to finish high school.

In eighth grade, they took me out of special ed, and the next year was difficult. I got straight Cs. But I got tutoring help, and I didn't go back into Special Ed.

All through these times, my mom was terrific. She was a great support. Although she had limited education, she always pushed me to try hard in school. Her goal was for me to graduate from high school and get a job. Given our educational history, that would have been ground-breaking.

I started to slack off in my eighth- and ninth-grade years. I partied, stopped doing my homework, and skipped school. This was probably due to the fact that my mom lost her job. Then she remarried, and that led to some additional tension at home. It was sort of weird. I was living at home, but I was very much on my own.

Also, I was still having some medical problems with speech and stuff, and I didn't have medical insurance. I got a job working at ACME supermarkets in the ninth grade (I worked there through high school and into college), and I got my medical insurance from them. So, I had my own health insurance at 16. I was taking care of myself and pretty proud of that. What a mindset for a 16-year-old! My mother called it "amazing." But going through all that really drove it home. I saw clearly that I never wanted to be powerless again. I was essentially on my own, and I needed to deal with that.

Sophomore and junior years, something clicked in school. I started understanding things better and getting B's. I doubled up classes and still did well. Frankly, I had all the credits I needed to graduate by the end of the 11th grade. But I stayed for the senior year. I went to school in the morning and worked jobs the rest of the time.

During my senior year, I qualified for a Senatorial scholarship to go to Cecil Community College, a local school. My mom was ecstatic, but I was pretty scared. No one else in my family had ever done this. As it turned out, math was still a problem, and I needed support. I struggled and dropped out after the first semester. Then, later, I enrolled at Wilmington University.

While trying to go to college all this time, I was still working at ACME. Then I got a second job at AAA. After AAA, I got a full-time job at Associate's Bank, which later was bought by CitiBank. It was my first full-time job. Life was good. I was making money, partying, you know the whole bit. For example, I wanted to buy a house, so I did.

But then, bing bang, 9/11 happened, I lost my job, and I had to stop going to Wilmington. It was awful. I had a mortgage to pay, and I was losing my car, losing everything, and my mom couldn't help in any meaningful way. I was powerfully reminded, once again, that I was on my own. I didn't know what to do, and the whole situation sort of broke my spirit. I was 21.

The next ten years or so were like the story of the revolving door. The good news was that I was never unemployed for long. I always got the job. The bad news was that I was always starting over. I had a succession of jobs, mostly at financial institutions like Bank of America, JP Morgan, Advance America, and Sallie Mae. The cycle repeated itself again and again. My problems were the lack of a degree, the glass ceiling I confronted as a Black man, and the fact that the financial markets were bad.

Then came the big turning point. I had been sort of sputtering around since 9/11. Surviving but not thriving, if you know what I mean. At the same time, at 28 in 2008, things were busy, and I was doing okay, but no forward progress. Then, in 2008, seeing Obama get elected President was huge for me. I said to myself, "if he can meet these challenges, so can I!" I got that old determination back and decided to go to college and work full-time.

The first step was to get an associate's degree from Strayer University in 2010. My sister also got her B.A. that year. Unbelievable. We were breaking the curses of generations in our family and for Black people in general. And I'd be lying if I said that there wasn't jealousy about what we were doing inside the family and out.

Then, Bank of America merged with another bank, and I lost my job again. I turned right around and applied for a job at JP Morgan Chase as a credit analyst. It turned out that this move opened up a huge door of opportunity. Among other things, I met my wife at that time. She had a B.A. and was working on an M.A. And she was always encouraging me to hang in there, to keep going. So, the question was: should I go to school and become an accountant or something? Or just keep working?

Once again, I lost my job in 2010. It was bizarre because I was going to propose to my girlfriend, and I purchased the engagement ring on that Friday. Then I lost my job on Monday. No way I was going to propose to her if I didn't have a job. I was very depressed.

I was unemployed and broke. I had to back out of my lease and move back into my aunt's house to save money. It was all backwards, the wrong direction. But I was determined not to let it defeat me. I knew I was smart, that I could do the work. At the same time, I realized that a lot of the jobs I wanted required a B.A. And I made a promise to myself to get the B.A. I was not going to start at the bottom every time.

The next year was amazing. I got a new job the following week through CareerBuilder (Advance America) and stayed there for a year. I also started school at Strayer, proposed to my girlfriend, and we got married. I was taking one class at a time until I got a better working schedule. But then I got a job at Discover, where they had a tuition reimbursement program. That was the good news. The bad news was that my federal financial aid was maxed out at that point. So, I just kept plugging along.

Then while I was at Discover, my wife had surgery. I was in the waiting area, and they called for "Code Blue." It was for her. When the doctor came out, I knew something was wrong. If she hadn't come in that day, she would have died. But she survived. But I had to delay school again just to cope with the situation and to get my head straight.

After my wife recovered, I was sort of marooned financially. I wanted to finish college, but I didn't want loans, my federal aid was maxed out, and the corporate support didn't cover all the costs. And then this magical thing happened. A woman was sitting next to my desk at work. I had never seen her before, and I never saw her again. She sat next to my desk one time, and she gave me this mind-blowing opportunity. She was a student at Strayer, so I was immediately interested in her story. She told me about this service called StraighterLine, where I could test out of any courses I could pass and get the credit transferred to Strayer. And the costs were a tiny fraction of Strayer's tuition, so it was definitely affordable.

For starters, I registered for a class just to get a feel for the whole thing. One weekend, I studied all weekend and then took the test on Sunday night. Bang! One course down, seven to go. I just knocked these courses off, completing eight in seven weeks. From all the jobs I had held, I just knew the stuff and passed the courses. Then I took and completed two classes at Strayer and graduated in 2017, the second person and first man in my family to get a B.A.

But even that victory had a sad downside. My father wouldn't come to my graduation. I don't know why for sure. But it felt like he was annoyed that I was trying to be "first" all the time. And I was the first man in my family to get a degree.

On top of all of that, in 2014, I had had a mini-stroke at work during my finals. And although I recovered, I had to stop out of college for a semester. It was crazy, tiring, emotional – all hell was breaking loose around me. That was the story of my life from my twenties into my thirties. Everything was happening. As they say, "life happened," intervening again and again. I was in survival mode. Then I got laid off, and the recession hit. But I got lucky and landed a job as a Child Support Specialist for the State of Delaware in 2015. And I just hung in there with Strayer.

But there were still some bumps in the road ahead. When I was with the state, I received the B.A. in 2017, and that gave me an opportunity. I applied for a promotion, and I got it. That made some people angry because I hadn't been there that long. But I was good at my job, so I got the next job. Then, within the next year, along came a senior manager job. I applied, but I didn't get it. I got beat out by a Caucasian woman with no B.A. What's that song, "You don't need a weatherman to know which way the wind is blowing?" It rubbed me the wrong way, and I started looking for another job, but this time with the B.A. in hand.

And I was getting my master's at the same time. Finished in 2019. I got straight A's all the way through. Not bad for a former special ed student who couldn't speak when he was five. I was 39 years old.

Then an amazing thing happened. One night, in the middle of the night, my cell phone buzzed. I answered it, and it was a job announcement. I got up right then and filled out the form. The next day I got a call for an interview that afternoon. I took the interview and thought I had done well. My personality helped as it had all through my life. Then the VP came into the room after the interview and offered me the job. This was only six months after getting my M.A. Here I was, able to help my family and make more money to support our future. After all, we have three kids, who are 11, 9, and 7, and I want a smoother road for them than the one I traveled.

As I look back, there are several factors that contributed to my ultimate success. Determination and my positive personality were door-openers. Employers always saw my determination. I wasn't into work cliques. I wanted to make money, and that required focus and productivity. I volunteered for extra duty, overtime, all those kinds of things. They always saw my leadership potential, but I didn't have the B.A., so I couldn't progress.

For example, at Discover, I filled in for and applied for a Quality Analyst position. But I never got the job. I applied for a whole bunch of jobs and didn't get one. I didn't have the degree, and I think that as a Black man, that was strike two. I learned early that determination and trying to learn every step of the way to do the work in front of me were key to success. But the B.A. opened the door.

And all that work I had done, all those jobs, came in really handy when I went back to school, even at the master's level. I was 39, but it was as if I had been training and prepping for the bachelor's and the master's for 20 years. I knew a lot of the stuff, just had to organize it a little differently.

And frankly, my faith journey was a big part of my learning as well. I always felt that God was looking out for me. Since I didn't have someone to pick up the phone, call, and get guidance from, I leaned on my faith, and that kept me going even when the going got tough. Even as a kid, my family was non-church, but I went to Sunday school on my own. I woke up one day, and off I went. Then, after a little time off, I went again in my twenties. The prodigal son returned.

Wrap it all up into one big ball, and I can see now that I learned from it all, both the bad and the good. And StraighterLine helped me over that last obstacle, affordability, on my way to the B.A. The rest is history. And the sky is the limit.

Jim Clemens

Jim lives with his husband and stepson in West Chester, Pa. He is a Certified Pharmacy Technician at Walmart in Exton, Pa. Jim says, "Somebody took a chance on me at Walmart, and that made the difference."

I had my IQ tested in first grade, and it was 110. They thought about advancing me, but then decided against doing that from a personal development point of view. I was advanced, but they wanted me to stay in sync with my age group. But, as smart as I was, school was a problem for me from the very beginning. And the same thing was true about work after I graduated from high school.

The trouble began my first day in first grade. I had a teacher who didn't like male students. As she put it, we "had to go out and work," and she thought she had to be hard on us. And she was even harder on me because, believe it or not, I was left-handed, and she thought left-handedness was a sin! So she tied my left hand down and made me write with my right hand.

I told my mother, and she confronted the teacher. They argued terribly, and my mom threatened her with a disciplinary complaint. Ultimately, she let me write with my left hand. But after the confrontation with my mother, the teacher treated me even worse.

Then, talk about bad luck, I got the same woman in the third grade, and things got worse. I developed a speech impediment which I now know resulted from the anxiety caused by her treatment. I got therapy, but it didn't work very well.

The anxiety, the speech impediment – all of it – stayed with me throughout school. I was in a gifted program in high school. But the nonsense never ended.

For instance, I had a 12th-grade teacher who asked me if I could read. I could read, but not out loud because of my condition. She actually said she didn't believe me, and she was going to fail me. Happily, that didn't happen. All my other teachers supported me, and I graduated.

I graduated from high school and went to work. The speech thing was crippling, really baked in. I was afraid to introduce myself, for instance, until I knew whether the other person would be friendly. Personally and professionally, it was bad.

I tried my hand at lots of jobs. But I continually had trouble, usually with women. I started at a bank. But the manager was an aggressive, over-bearing person, and she didn't like me. I was fired because the bank had been taken over, and they were eliminating jobs. But I thought she had an ulterior motive.

Then I got an office job at an insurance company in the inner city. I was a clerk in a nine-to-five job. This time I got another woman supervisor. She was older, and we had a misunderstanding which she took the wrong way. She conspired with two other people to set me up – said I was domineering and rude. If they had succeeded in firing me for cause, I would have been unemployable. So, I went to personnel because I wasn't going to let them ruin my reputation. When the personnel director saw the termination for cause letter, she tore it up. She said they'd help me get unemployment benefits if I resigned. So, I had to resign to avoid the destruction of my reputation. At the time, one of the accusers called me "chickenshit" for not facing them and fighting back. But the personnel people saved me.

Next, I went to a temp agency and got another office job, insurance again, as part of a group of clerks. I was 24 and that's when I started at Peirce Junior College as a part-time student in the evenings. I was going for an associate's degree in Computer Science. It took me four years, but I finally hit my stride academically with a 4.0 average the first year. There wasn't any of the drama that I had in elementary and high school. Night students, so-called non-traditional students, and the people who taught us were very different. We all had day jobs, and the environment was professional. Importantly, all our professors were there to help, not challenge.

I got my associate's in Applied Science with a 3.5 GPA in Computer Science. I am very proud that I broke new ground there. I insisted that evening students be included on the honor roll, and they changed the policy in January 1999.

I then tried my hand in industry, but the rule there was not "what you know, but who you know." I had opportunities, but people were asking me to do what they wanted, not what the job description said and what I knew and wanted to do. I was looking for a challenge, and they were boring me. It was a bait and switch. IT was a small field at that time. I could have gotten a leg up if I had an "in." But I didn't.

The anxiety and speech issues were still there, but things got even more complicated. I came to understand that I was gay and came out to my parents. That helped a little because both my mom and my grandmother were very supportive and asked, "What took you so long?"

I decided to try another line of work because even though I had my AAS, I was still essentially a mail clerk. This started a series of contract jobs in personal computing and related work. My first job lasted a year. It was great. I controlled the time and could work on the task at hand. I loved getting done early and having the afternoon to myself. I started to work out and take care of myself. I was in shape physically and mentally. But the bottom line was that contract work was good for flexibility but bad because there was no progression at all.

So, I was 36 or 37, and I wanted to finish college, but there was no opportunity. I went to work at a print shop in Delaware. I was hired as a temp and proved myself, so I got the full-time job. But it was 2008, and the economy was going south. Ultimately, my employer had to terminate me. Ironically, it happened on my 40th birthday in 2010.

Being afraid of making a mistake, taking blame, and believing my impediment was my fault and the resulting anxiety over all those years was enormous. When I lost that printing job, that was the final straw. I had a nervous breakdown in 2009.

Amazingly, the breakdown was a transition event, a reset of my entire life. I recovered and got counseling. I learned not to deal with people who are putting me down, pestering me. It was, it sounds strange, the best thing that happened to me. I let all of the anxiety go. Then the counseling paid off when I realized that ever since the first grade, I had been bullied by authority figures. So, at 38, the tide turned. I started getting serious about my anxiety and the meds that help assuage it. My speech, as well as my anxiety, improved. It turned out that I had social anxiety as well as general anxiety.

In 2010, I started my own business, becoming a certified personal fitness trainer. I enjoyed it. I controlled how much I worked, my clients, and my income. Also, I worked at a club. The manager there really helped me learn the business, from marketing to pricing to managing other trainers. I was a fitness trainer and manager until 2017. By then, I had done everything I could do, and the challenge of the work was ebbing. Once again, I was bored.

So, I went to work at a retail establishment, we catered to hair stylists and aestheticians. The manager hired me because of my business background, but she was very passive-aggressive with me. I was a customer service manager, and she set standards that were impossible. I felt absolutely that it had to do with my LGBTQ status. And to be truthful, I did have a bit to learn about the business. But after my counseling and turnaround, I wasn't going to put up with it.

I had started with counseling because I got to a point where I needed to get a handle on the speech thing if I was going to solve the problem. The doctor and the counselor helped me understand that the root cause was anxiety that stemmed from all the crap I took in elementary school. The diagnosis, a little counseling, and daily medication years later have made the difference.

I am a different person because of the solution and the acceptance of a mental health diagnosis as being societally legitimate and not something to hide or worry about, especially for men. It is not something to be ashamed of. It is a fact of life.

The current chapter of my life opened in late 2017 when I landed at Walmart. I started as a part-time cashier in Exton and worked my way up through customer service desk host to manager in less than a year.

At the same time, I had heard about Live Better University (LBU), a Walmart education benefit in 2018. If you enrolled and stayed in good standing, you paid a dollar a day, and they paid the rest after financial aid was taken into account. Available programs were Business, Management and Leadership, and supply-chain management. I did my research, and I applied to Bellevue University, got accepted, and began in January 2019 in Business Management and Leadership.

The online aspect of Bellevue was good for me. I really didn't have time to go to a campus. You work at your own pace, manage your own time, the faculty is very responsive, and counseling is available. And I was able to transfer almost all my Associate Degree credits, and that was very helpful, saving me a lot of time.

Back in my other life, the Exton store hired an assistant manager who didn't like me. She imposed all sorts of expectations and goals on me, and she tried to break me, but I wouldn't let her. I had learned not to take that crap. Ultimately, I transferred to another store in Parkesburg, Pa. as a department manager. It wasn't a good fit, so I was transferred to customer service as self-checkout host, a significant cut in pay and a step backward, to say the least.

After the demotion, I called the manager of the pharmacy in the Exton store, who I knew and liked, and asked if she had an opening. She said she did, and I told her I'd take it. I returned to the Exton store in March 2020 to work in the pharmacy, a challenge that I really wanted and needed. I got hired as a Pharmacy Technician in March 2020, and along with the Bellevue course work I was already doing, I took an internal course in Pharmacy Tech, finishing in May 2020. After that, I earned my national certification at the end of November 2020.

My education at Bellevue has helped my pharmacy work enormously. Everything I have learned in the courses is practical, and I can use it right away. So, I manage the business and help the manager with scheduling, training, merchandising, inventory, technical support, and related business activities.

I remember when I was a kid that my grandma, age 65, went back to finish high school. I asked my mom, "isn't she too old?" My grandma got tears in her eyes, and Mom told me, "you are never too old to learn!" And she ordered me to go hug her. I never forgot it, and it became a great motivator for me. As I looked back, I said to myself, "If she could do that, so can I." And my dad never finished high school. That was his one goal for us all. Seeing what he experienced with a tenth-grade education was a motivator as well.

Think of it this way. I am just a number to Walmart, one of tens of thousands, if not millions, of employees. But they are willing to pay all my education costs after I pay a dollar a day. That's amazing. I will graduate in June 2021. Looking ahead, I want to give back to Walmart by moving up and influencing younger associates to see the opportunities available.

Ron Williams

Ron Williams is married and the father of 2 children. He is an Operations Associate at the McDonald's Corporation He evaluates all aspects of roughly 100 stores in northern California and Nevada, including customer satisfaction, quality, cleanness, service, and safety.

In order to really understand my journey, you've got to go back to the very beginning. All I remember in my earliest years was just me and my mom living in Section 8 housing in Oakland. My mom was wonderful. But she had to work all the time. So, as a preschooler, I spent a whole lot of time with other relatives. I had no sense of my dad at all. He was invisible, not present. Occasionally he'd call, like on my birthday or at Christmas. But where he was calling from was never clear and not discussed.

Then, one day my auntie took me for a car ride. I was maybe five at the time. We went into this huge old gray building with fences around it, and she told me that it was a "penitentiary" where he was staying. The full meaning of it didn't hit me for quite a while. But there he was, behind a glass wall in an orange jump suit with a phone in his hand. I remember touching the glass, and then he said, "I am your dad."

In a way, it didn't mean anything right then because I didn't really understand. But after he was released, he would appear from time to time and try to make amends. So, I figured out who he was, literally, but he was never part of my life, and my sense of him was very negative. What I didn't know at the time was that he was in a drug gang, on the streets, and doing no good, to put it mildly. I learned that a little later. But then that whole thing was resolved when he was killed, gunned down in broad daylight, in the streets of Oakland.

You get this sense of being a victim, staying with relatives, going to Oakland schools. I always had a desire to learn. But there was no flow, no pattern. It was never clear just how everything worked.

I was starting school at that point. And, you know, it's funny in a weird way. I was really good at school academically, but the whole thing was filled with tension. I had problems with a lot of the other kids. We were all in the same situation: poor, single parents, crime everywhere. But most of them were headed in a different direction. And there I was – smart, shy – so I was the target of a lot of bullying during those years. I played sports to show I was tough. Although I still gravitated to education on the inside, I just couldn't act that way.

As I look back on it, there were two pathways: fit in with the gang and get in trouble or use education as the way out. It was like a life lottery, but I couldn't just beat the odds and win it with a ticket. Education was something I could control, and it was the only way out. So that's the path I chose.

When I was seven, my mom got married, and my dad, I have called him Dad ever since, has been in my life ever since. He was a very different kind of person, including that he was present all the time in a very positive way. He was more geared towards self-improvement. And he always pushed college even though he never went himself. Here's a good example which I have never forgotten. I had gotten in some trouble. And after he had scolded me, he gave me an article called "Critical Thinking" and told me to read it and write him a report about it. He wanted me to take myself seriously!

Eventually, we moved to Paterson in northern California. That was a total game-changer. I was a Black kid in a Mexican-white school. And the community was way more suburban; the parents were generally better educated, and they stressed discipline and getting ahead. It was a whole different environment.

Gradually I got my arms around this new deal, and it slowly started to change my outlook, my dress, and my behavior. Then a series of positive things began to happen. Mr. Thompson, my guidance counselor, signed me up for the National Youth State Leadership Conference. I asked him "why," and he said, "I see something in you." This was so foreign to me. I didn't know what leadership was, but I had people saying, "I see something in you." At the same time, my parents couldn't really afford extra help for me, including the leadership conference. In fact, Mom and I went from church to church to raise the money to send me to San Jose for the meeting. But by god, I got there! It was a pretty interesting situation. There was lots of positive attention, and I began to see leadership as more than a word.

In high school, I was in all honor roll classes, like 3.8 average. I had a teacher, Mr. Ojeda, in Algebra, who was paralyzed from the waist down. One day he asked if anyone could help him at home; that, given his paralysis, he needed a little help around the house. I showed up and helped. I made some money and felt useful and giving. To this day, we are close friends.

I asked about his paralysis, and he told me all about it. He had had a vibrant and active life. But then he got a tumor in his spine, which caused the paralysis. He told me it was devastating at the time. But over time, he decided that he wasn't going to let life take away his education and his mind. It's like go with what you've got. Here I had showed up to help out, and I got a huge lesson in courage and strength. It was very inspirational.

Then things went south for a while. The summer before senior year, one of my brother's friends was murdered by his father. He was also a close friend of mine. We all went to church together. They had seemed to be a happy family, and I really struggled with it. At the same time, my girlfriend dumped me, and I was just having problems sorting it all out. One of my reactions was to act out at home. So, I was not getting along with the family either.

Having grown up with no dad, this really hit me and my sense of purpose. I ran away to my aunt's house, about a mile away. Then I got cut from basketball, and that only added fuel to the fire. I had friends, and I felt cool, and then that was gone. I started having a "whatever" mentality and started partying and all that. I was doing this to myself, a lot of it.

It's hard to balance that kind of behavior with being a good student, like trying to live a double life. I had been in the AVID program for all four years. It was a support program for first-generation college students giving them access to the information you need to get into college. Mr. Bettencourt was my AVID teacher for all four years. And when he saw my grades coming down and my attitude changing, he confronted me. With tears in his eyes, he said, "I'm not going to let you go back where you came from!" And when he confronted me, that was a turning point. I turned it all around, graduated, and went to Cal State Stanislaus.

After graduation from high school, I was in a unique situation, to put it mildly. My second dad made a good income, but my mom was stay-at-home, and there were five kids, including me. So, his income was too good for me to qualify for federal financial aid or Cal Grants, but I needed to look for other sources to pay for college. My parents wouldn't sign for a loan, so I had to do that. I was a Bio Major, and there was a lot of work. Then, during my second year, the cost of books, transportation (I couldn't do special projects because of the bus schedule), and food became unbearable. I was in a real jam, and I knew that I had to get a job. So, during the summer, I got a job at McDonald's. It slowed down my progress at school, but I had to do it. Then, in my fifth and sixth years, I benefited from Archways to Opportunity. It allowed me to stop worrying about money and get a better balance between school and work with and more focus on academics.

Getting into Archways was totally happenstance. Actually, it is sort of a funny story. One day at work, Teri Regalado, the owner-operator, told me about how her daughter was about to graduate from college. I told her the same was true for me. She did a double-take and said, "You're in college?" Then she took me under her arm and told me about Archways, a program at McDonald's which provides financial support and guidance for employees to go to college. She brought me to her office and got me signed up for tuition assistance. This saved my butt. I was close to the end, but I was really hurting, and I needed the money to buy books.

I was 22, it was 2016, and I graduated in 2017 with a B.A. in Micro-Biology. It's sort of ironic. You go to college for six years, get a biology degree and end up in the business of hospitality. I love hospitality, and I love people, and the combination of my work experience and employable skills with college knowledge was really great. The two together created a new Ronald, that's me, a guy who had a higher meaning and purpose because of both.

As I look back on it all, my curiosity as a kid played all the way through. I learned about operations, technology, and all the things that go on behind the scenes because I kept asking questions and poking around. They are essential to making the business run, and you need to know about them to be successful.

Also, when I was still in college, I knew there was the importance of first impressions. My father used to say, "you only get one chance to make a first impression." At the restaurant, that mattered, so I let my personality shine through.

Then one day at McDonald's, two guys who worked for the company came into the store. I was introduced to them, and as I spoke with them, I realized that I would really like to work for the company as a career. I told them my dreams about working for the company, but nothing happened. No help there. So, I took care of it myself. I found a contact and connected with a guy named Ronald at corporate McDonald's (can you believe it, two Ronalds at McDonald's?). I sent him an email, stated my desire, and he forwarded the email to team members and also to HR. I stayed after them, contacting HR bi-weekly, and my persistence was rewarded. Finally, a job opened, and I got an interview and the job the same day.

All these people—my dad, Mr. Thompson, Mr. Ojeda, Mrs. Regalado, my mom, and the Archways program—helped me collectively in a way that I could never have helped myself.

Now, I have been in corporate for two years. And, as I look ahead, I am interested in leadership. All the way back to Mr. Thompson in middle school, people see leadership in me, and I feel it as well. I want to have an impact on others' lives, make those lives better through leadership and personal development.

One thing I've learned is that every bad situation in your life, every struggle, challenge, disappointment, set back are all learning opportunities. For example, when my father died, I learned about there being a better way. My father's death was, in retrospect, a real turning point.

I got married the year I graduated and am now the father of two amazing kids. With the lesson of the father who wasn't there and then the experience of being supported by my second father, the greater lessons in life matter to me. To be there, to be positive, to give them more opportunity. I learned about pushing for the future. That's what I live for.

Now we are living in Modesto. I work in the corporate office in Walnut Creek, doing evaluations of stores, customer satisfaction evaluation—quality, cleanness, service- safety, clean equipment. My service area spans about 100 stores in northern California and into Nevada. It is a lot of driving but really fun. I am an Operations Associate, which means there is a manager above me. I do the day-to-day work, and I am shooting for manager next.

And college is still part of our lives. Presently, my wife is at home with the kids and getting her B.A. in Psychology at Southeastern University. And I am currently enrolled in a master's program at Colorado Tech in Organizational Leadership. I am still practicing what I learned from Mr. Bettencourt back in school. It turned out that he had actually dropped out of school before returning, finishing, and becoming a teacher. He said, "The choices you make today will affect your tomorrow." That's what I live by.

Even though I had a tough start, I learned persistence, motivation, hard work, respect, and humility; I learned that life has its ups and downs, but things will work out if you stay at it. I learned from life experience, and it paid off.

Colleges That Helped

Jose Rodriguez

Jose Rodriguez is in his mid-thirties. He is the Director of Prison Education and Assistant Director of Recruitment at College UnBound in Providence, Rhode Island.

To set the scene, I dropped out of middle school in the seventh grade. We lived in the projects. And every day, my walk to the school bus stop was through a never-ending crime story of drugs and prostitution. Prostitution and drug dealing were the daily realities.

On that particular day, a pimp was beating his prostitute right there on the corner. The pimp had his gun out and, as a result, my school bus driver decided not to stop, leaving me behind with nowhere to go. He was probably worried about the safety of the kids on the bus. But there I was, stuck and in danger myself, with no one to protect me. It sort of flipped a switch in me, and I decided that nobody cared about any kid from the projects and certainly not me. I was not expected to do anything good with life anyway, so what the hell.

Then I just sort of started to drift. I decided that, since I was going to be a failure anyway, the world that school represented really didn't matter. I dropped out before the end of the seventh grade and eventually fell in with the gangs and the drug dealers. There were two paths available to a kid like me, and the situation with the bus driver that day put me on the other path. The gangs were my network and support.

The next several years were a cycle of being in and out of juvenile detention. And since I was rebelling against regular education, the folks there said that I should think about a trade. Because in that world, you've got to do something. If you don't want to go to school, you need to get a trade. So, I chose barbering.

But barbering or no barbering, as I cycled through the juvenile system, things got more extreme. Eventually, I began to rely on a gun to get my way. I never really thought about using it, but it was handy because nobody messes with you when you are holding a gun.

But more trouble was inevitable. When I was 19, I shot a man and went to prison. with a five-to-ten-year sentence. There I was, in jail, with no prospects for success or redemption. But then this little miracle happened. I had had a child when I was 15, a daughter. One day, after about a year, I got a visit from my daughter and her mom. At one point, my daughter, a five-year-old, said, "Daddy, when you get out, if you go back to jail, I won't love you anymore."

That was that. I couldn't imagine letting my daughter down. All of a sudden, I was looking for every training program available and any other activities that would get me "good time" and my sentence reduced. Education was one of the routes I followed. First, I got my GED, and then I looked for more. The Community College of

Rhode Island (CCRI) was offering courses, and I started taking them. I'm not sure how great they were, but they began to prepare me for college. I had been out of school, other than barber school, since the seventh grade, and I was way behind. Math, reading, writing, forget it. But I began to try.

The good news is that my turn-around did get me "good time," and that led to a shorter term. When I got out of prison, I chose to stay on the path, to go straight. I took a job at the Institute for the Study and Practice of Non-violence in Providence. The Executive Director there, Teny Gross, took a gamble on me and gave me a job when he didn't actually have the funding for it. His philosophy is about recycling human capital and putting behavior that had hurt the community in service to help the community. That sparked the change that I am living today.

At the time, I was thinking that it would be a good thing to give back to the community and help other kids avoid the pit I had fallen into. But even as I began work and really got into it, I had this suspicion that, with my back story, there were going to be limits on how far I could go without more education. I was going to be explaining myself continually without the protection of a degree. I needed more education.

I enrolled again in the CCRI and took a couple of courses, including a communications course. The way it worked, I had to write a report on a subject and then do an oral presentation on what I had written. Well, since I didn't know how to write, I wrote the way I spoke. It was a real mess. At the end of the class, the professor gave me the paper back, told me it was terrible, and suggested that I not pursue an academic career. He didn't offer to help or give guidance on how to improve. He just brushed me off. I was crushed.

This was in 2011-12, and College UnBound (CU) had just begun. Whether it was divine intervention or pure luck, the Institute for the Practice of Non-Violence, where I worked, had a board member who was also on the CU board. One day CU's Provost, Adam Bush, came by to tell the Institute staff about it and see if we could build it into what we were doing in the community.

I liked what I heard and enrolled in 2013, one of eight people in the cohort. Three years later, I completed the degree program successfully.

The CU program was organized around project work. And working at the Institute, my job was to find creative ways to prevent violence, a project-based approach. So, my job became my learning plan, and my learning activities became my job.

It wasn't like a traditional college at all. They had core courses to help you to identify a project. The things I had started at the Institute were not aggressive enough, so I had to get another project helping the folks in the community I was working with. Having been trained as a barber, I noticed that a lot of the kids needed haircuts. Bad hair can make you feel crappy. So, I started a barber shop where we would cut kids' hair for free and, while we were doing it, we discussed non-violence. It was sort of a club in the barber shop.

College was actually fun and very rewarding because I was doing what I wanted to do, and everything was in that framework. Now the math courses were supporting what I was doing, the writing and logistics were all supporting me to do a better job leading the project. I had to figure out grants, so I learned how to write better because it was cause-oriented, and I was passionate. Purpose-driven learning was what it was.

We met at the high school at night. Why not? It was empty. CU gave me some advanced placement for the credit I had earned in jail. And you had to do an assessment of prior learning. That was a ten-page paper, highlighting how you met the requirements for a specific course. So, for example, as supervisor of the street outreach program, I could use that experience to meet some course outcomes.

I started in the spring of '13, and I was awarded associate degree in the spring of '14. Using and then building on my life experience, it took me just one year to earn 60 credits. My daughter was starting high school, and I wanted to show her.

I was slated to finish the B.A. in a year, but I got in trouble and went back to prison later in 2014. It was a technical violation, not reporting to my probation officer. I was busy, and I forgot. Also, I was doing good things in the community and staying out of trouble. But they simply ignored all that and sent me away for 15 months.

I was in a "not good" mood at this point. But then CU began their in-prison program. It was lucky timing for me. I had had some good luck and some bad luck along the way, to put it mildly. And I had already taken the courses they were offering. But I was able to become a college mentor to the inmates in the program because I had already completed the coursework they were taking. When CU brought the idea to me, I jumped at it. And it kept me busy, productive, and feeling useful for the rest of my term. When I got out in late '15, I went back to the Institute. I didn't go back to CU till the fall of '17, and I graduated in the spring of '18. And, yes, I got some credit for the mentoring I had done with the other students while I was in jail.

After I graduated, I became director of a family shelter, but the bureaucracy at the place was killing me. They were always looking over my shoulder and putting forms and reports ahead of service. I was doing some counseling with Dennis, president of CU, and he suggested that maybe the shelter, as important as it was, might not be the right place for me. The next day he hired me. Now I work for CU as Director of Prison Education and Assistant Director of recruitment.

Looking back on all the things that have happened, I have learned a few things about myself. I am passion driven. It is easier for me if I believe that a job and the organization I work for will have positive outcomes. I am a good supervisor-leader, and the CU program reinforces my abilities to play to my strengths. Now, I know I was exercising those natural abilities in my projects. But the program taught me to understand them more clearly and know them in a more concrete way.

Now they have a course called "restructuring failure." Through it, they teach you how to look at failures in your life through the "glass-half-full" lens. They ask how you might use the learning from those failures to achieve success in upcoming settings. For me, it was my natural affinity to lead and to communicate with different audiences. But let's do it to achieve something good the next time.

My daughter has been crucial to my success several times. When I got out of jail, she was entering middle school. We all know that's when problems can happen. And it is also when I first got into trouble. As background, her mom hadn't graduated from high school, nor had anyone else in either of our families. Also, several cousins and family members had become teen mothers. I wanted to model for her, to be a positive example. I had the GED, but I wanted to succeed at college for myself as well as for her. My thought was, "If you want to break the cycle, you got to start somewhere." Currently, she is a student at Rhode Island College. And when she graduates, that will be a red-letter day for my family and for her.

As I look back, I had three teachers who changed my life: my daughter when she told me she wouldn't love me if I screwed up again, Teny Gross, who believed in me and shared his philosophy with me, and College UnBound, which gave me a voice for my learning.

Anna Raymond

Anna Raymond is a Research Specialist in Pulmonary and Critical Care at the University of Vermont.

To this day, I recommend assessing your prior and personal learning to anyone I see or speak with who expresses an interest in returning to school as an adult learner. What a great learning opportunity, especially if you are like me; an adult single parent who was a little anxious about re-entering college and unsure sure of what she really knew. Perhaps you have worked hard, raised kid(s), and lived a full life, but what is it worth when it comes to getting a new job or a promotion? And what is it worth at the local college? That recognition could be worth time and money because you get advanced standing and save time towards a degree.

Having said that, and in retrospect, I had a pretty good sense of what I already knew. From a business degree perspective, I had practicum credits and business degree credits in areas like billing and coding, word processing, computer work, and patient documentation.

For example, I once received a promotion and needed to learn about billing very quickly. I checked with my organization to see what they could offer in terms of training and support. The hospital provided me with a training session and reference materials for basic outpatient billing. While much of that learning was trial and error over the following months, being willing to research billing protocols and policies on my own was key to learning the skills I needed to perform the job successfully.

If questioned, many people would not know the answer to *"What college-level skills have I learned on the job, or from life?"* If you are looking to return to school and are unsure where to begin, I would recommend listing all the jobs you have performed in your life and drill down on what talents those jobs required and how they may relate to college-level learning. It has been my experience that the people you work with, and for, that are experts in their respective fields are more than willing to speak to your level of experience and education while creating the letters of support needed for the Assessment of Prior Learning course.

In my case, I knew that my 20 years of work experience was valuable and that I brought a wealth of knowledge with me. I had moved through a number of departments and positions over the years, gaining experience in both the inpatient areas and outpatient clinics. My work covered Registration, Customer Service, Surgical Scheduling and Hospital Billing, as well as becoming a Licensed Nursing Assistant in the Medical Intensive Care Unit.

As part of the Assessment of Prior Learning course, I reviewed the syllabi of courses and was confident that I would be able to prove the knowledge required to earn those course and practicum credits! Workplace communication, working in a professional environment, and teamwork are all skills you may hone over years on the job. Professionalism is not only taught in a classroom, and college is able to teach things that you cannot learn on the job. Having said all that, I must admit that the enhanced value and respect that I felt after the validation of my personal learning was huge.

So, how did I get where I am? I did well in high school, and I always planned to go to college. I was in the National Honor Society, and I knew I would need financial aid to go. I applied to a handful of schools and received a full scholarship to Johnson and Wales in Providence, Rhode Island.

That year was an experience for me. Providence was a big city and far from home, two things I had little experience with. My grades were okay but not spectacular. The following year I was offered another scholarship, although a smaller one. I came home during the summer and got a job at the hospital after weeks of applying all over town. By the time I received my first paycheck, the summer was almost over. I made the decision to defer a year to earn the money I would need to pay for school. That one year turned into two decades, and I never went back.

Fast forward 20 years. I was nearly 40, a single mother, and I interviewed for a position at the hospital in an outpatient clinic. The woman conducting the interview had recently completed the assessment of prior learning course at the Community College of Vermont. She was finishing her bachelor's degree in Business Management. And she was looking forward to earning her master's degree. She was adamant that I should also take advantage of the program offering after reviewing my resume. Her excitement made me consider returning to the classroom after so many years away.

I accepted the job, settled in, and received a promotion to a mid-level position after about six months. There was a steep learning curve while I accustomed myself to the surgical specialty in an office that was fast-paced. I genuinely enjoyed the work and patient population. Hard work and a pleasant demeanor taken together go a long way. The manager who interviewed me moved on to a new position shortly after my hire, but I never stopped thinking about her enthusiastic encouragement that I should take the APL course. I had just committed to enrolling when the hospital announced a limited number of grants to cover the cost of taking the APL course. It felt like a sign. I applied and received one of the grants. It was 2016.

I ultimately received 54 credits. I was thrilled to learn I only had five classes left to get my degree, and after three semesters, I had it.

Returning to college to earn a degree was part of a longer-term plan to make sure that I locked in my son's opportunity to earn an advanced degree without being saddled with debt. I wanted to plan for his college as well as my own. I updated my resume and started applying at the University of Vermont College of Medicine. UVM offers tuition relief for dependents and tuition reimbursement for employees. Leaving the hospital after nearly 25 years was certainly out of my comfort zone, but I wanted the security of finishing the B.A. and giving my son an incredible opportunity, as well.

I have now worked around physicians and scientists with advanced degrees in the health care world since I was nineteen. It is a humbling thing to work among people focused on scientific discovery and patient care. Though I will never likely complete a Ph.D. program, I am more motivated than ever to meet them where they are at. I cannot imagine leaving UVM, as there are so many opportunities available, both educational and professional.

It certainly was a long road to the associate degree that I finally got at the Community College of Vermont. But I am grateful for the path that led me there and even I more grateful for the manager that saw untapped potential in me and encouraged me to join. I sing the praises of the APL opportunity to anyone I meet that voices an interest in returning to college as an adult learner. In the years since, I have been invited back to speak with incoming students about the work that is required to earn 54 credits in a single semester; that work is hard but so incredibly valuable.

Andrew Wheatley

Andrew Wheatley is a naturalized citizen, having immigrated from Jamaica in 2000. He served years active duty in the Marine Corps and is currently a member of the Marine Corps Reserves. At 36, he recently graduated from the University of Maryland Global Campus and is looking for his next opportunity.

I was born in Kingston, Jamaica and, after living my early years in the countryside, I moved to Kingston for elementary school. If there is one narrative for my years in Jamaica, it is that I was a loner, the weird kid. Despite being tall and athletic, the thought of playing basketball never really interested me. I usually viewed my surroundings much differently than my peers. I was more inclined to analyze the situation before taking certain logical action.

Even with my cousins, I was usually the odd one out. But my parents never tried to stifle me. They took some flack because I was "different." But they let me be who I was. My father was a disciplinarian. But whether I was messing with broken electronics or taking an old TV apart, he let me be. Hanging around bad company or just chilling outside in the yard at night was forbidden. Those rules most likely saved my life, as many of my buddies did not make it to adulthood.

My mother was the same way. She knew that I was choosing to be different, and she did her best to make things easier. I always had a deep interest in electronics and computers, although I never grew up owning one. That changed when I was 14, and my mother brought home a dusty old Windows 3.x pc. We had no idea if it would work or how to operate it, but I somehow managed to figure it out and get it up and running.

In school, I was very technical and excelled in the sciences on many levels. After skipping the fifth grade, my sixth-grade teacher nicknamed me "Mad Scientist." Math and literature always seemed to elude me and did not grasp my interest. I continued to take electronics apart and fix them. I had no idea of what to do when I started. I just played with them, broke them down, and fixed them.

In my early teens, Cartoon network, Sci-Fi, ZDTV, and Discovery channel were mainly what I would consume on TV. Anything science-related, whether science fiction or science fact, pricked my interest even more.

I had my eyes on the military from a pretty young age. In primary school, I was in the cub scouts. Then while attending high school, I joined the Jamaica Combined Cadet Force (JCCF). The goal was to graduate and eventually join the defense force or the British Royal Marines.

I was about six months from graduating when things changed. My grandmother had filed for us, and we were accepted to come to America on a green card. The window was limited, so in December 2000, I boarded a flight from my home in Jamaica to Brooklyn, NY. I never imagined how missing those six months would affect me going forward.

I started attending Cobble Hill High School in Brooklyn but was told that I had to start over from scratch. The Jamaican and American school systems were very different. The Jamaican education system is primarily modeled from the British system. So, at age 16, I was back in the ninth grade.

One day I found a small computer lab upstairs in the school. It was for elective classes such as graphic design and digital music. I went back up there after school to learn more about these classes. Ms. Kelly, the teacher, was extremely welcoming, and her wealth of knowledge was impressive. So, I became a regular up there. One day after school, I was playing around with a 3d program called 3ds Max 4, and instantly fell in love. I picked it up extremely quickly and was constantly learning new things while being challenged. Eventually, it became an elective class for 3d modeling and animation that I attended and naturally excelled at.

I still remember the day I was tasked with creating a simple tutorial, so that anyone could pick up and use the computer program with zero knowledge. That tutorial was used by members of the Board of Education to test the feasibility of continuing the program and updating the aging computers. They loved it! Needless to say, I was excited to see these not-smiling people looking like kids in a candy store. It was a simple table and chair tutorial, and I was told it made them feel young again.

When I was a sophomore, I was still thinking about what military branch I wanted to enlist in. At first, it was between the Army and the Air Force. But then a friend of mine mentioned the Marine Corps. I immediately researched them, but unknown to me, my friend had told his recruiter about my interest. The recruiter called me, and we had a short conversation for a future appointment. At first, I was not really feeling it, but and my mom said that I should at least listen to what he had to say.

I told my recruiter that high school was not working out and that I was going to get my GED. He advised against it and helped me transfer to City-As-School. It featured project-based and external learning. I ended up working on the USS Intrepid as an intern for credits towards graduation while doing other school projects and getting ready for the military. At this point, I made the decision to enlist in the Marine Corps.

While earning credits towards graduating, I was inducted into the poolee program. A poolee is an individual who has already signed up to become a Marine but has not yet left for boot camp. While preparing for the ASVAB, my math score was not the best. But my recruiter and other poolees helped and tutored each other to get where we all needed to be.

My math eventually improved, and I did pretty well on the ASVAB and qualified as an Aviation Mechanic. In January 2005, at age 20, I graduated from City-as-School with my high school diploma. I was ecstatic. Two weeks later, I was on my way to Parris Island for basic training. I was on active duty for nine years and, along the way, I earned my citizenship in 2009.

I started my college journey while I was deployed to Djibouti. My Chief Warrant Officer recommended that I attend college in order to not waste my potential. First, I attended American Military University. Things were steady in the beginning, but then operations started to ramp up. The teachers knew we were overseas and usually worked with us even when we had spotty internet.

This all changed during my Psychology class. I was doing very well until we had an internet outage that lasted a few days. When the internet came back, the professor refused to accept or grade my final paper. This left a bad taste in my mouth, and I decided not to continue taking classes at that school. After returning to the US, I started to attend Ashford University. But that did not last too long either because my military workload started ramping up.

While on my second deployment, I was selected to become a Marine Corps recruiter. Unfortunately, when the time came for me to attend recruiting school, everything stopped. The force began to do a rapid shrink and was not allowing many sergeants to re-enlist. My school orders were canceled, and I was afforded 30 days to process out of active duty. Fortunately, I had the option to transfer to the reserves.

It was a dark and difficult time for me, but I was undeterred. After shaking off the depression of suddenly leaving active duty, I got back to work. I stayed in California and found the only reserve MV22 osprey unit available. I started to feel alive again on my drill weekends. I also started driving for Uber and Lyft and actually enjoyed it.

I needed a career change, and something more permanent since going back on active duty was not an option available to me. I then discovered CompTIA and their IT certifications. I decided to give college another try and attended California Institute of Arts and Technology (CIAT). I took two classes then left because the advertised services did not align with the actual learning process.

I started ramping up my rideshare work and self-studies. In between rideshare trips, I would study the exam objectives while reading and watching videos on the topics. It all paid off when I passed the exams for the A+ and Network+ certifications on the first attempt. The learning process made me realize what I was missing and exposed me to new technologies.

About two years later, I started to ponder a commission in the U.S. Navy as an Information Professional (IP) officer. It requires a Bachelor of Science degree in certain computer-related technical fields and a 3.5 GPA. I then decided to use that as the catalyst to push me to complete an eligible degree program. I started looking long and hard and decided to do an orientation.

I went to National University's orientation, and all seemed well. In the classroom, the question about credit transfers was the topic of conversations. I mentioned that I held both A+ and Network+ certifications but was told I would not get credits for them since I did not take official related classes at a college. This perplexed me since the IT classes were designed to prep us for these certifications. I quickly decided against that school and never looked back.

I then remembered a few years back in passing, a female Marine had mentioned UMUC, which was the old name of University of Maryland Global Campus (UMGC). It had slipped my mind up until that point. I looked them up and was impressed. Surprisingly, they were having an open house as well in a few days. I signed up and went. I explained my situation and desired goals, and was blown away by the level of care and understanding.

Renetta Watts and Diane Topping were rock stars. Before I even agreed to attend the school, they evaluated my transcripts from the military and past institutions. This gave me a clear idea of what was most likely to transfer when the official transcript came. I was also informed that I would receive credits for both my A+ and Network+ certifications. This pretty much sealed the deal, and I started the admissions process before leaving.

Since my goal was to earn a high GPA, I quit driving and devoted myself to the singular purpose of earning my degree as quickly as possible. I used the GI bill, which allowed me to focus on taking multiple classes simultaneously while not worrying about my bills. When the pandemic started, UMGC was already prepared since their classes were already designed to be taught online or in a hybrid setting.

Due to the eight-week format and taking multiple classes simultaneously, it was very difficult and stressful, especially the tech classes. Fortunately, my nerd brain was up for the challenge. I took classes on Cybersecurity, Linux, Cisco CCNA, Microsoft Server, digital forensics, and many more. Capable professors helped to keep me grounded and challenged me to keep pushing.

On December 19, 2020, I graduated from UMGC with my Bachelor of Science in Computer Networks and Cybersecurity. I earned my 4.0 GPA and was inducted into the Phi Kappa Phi honor society. I continued to self-study, and in late January 2021, I passed my CompTIA Security+ certification exam on the first attempt.

Right now, I am working on some home projects and my resume. I am monitoring the pandemic and how that will affect my transition and commission to the Navy. I am also keeping an eye out for UMGC's upcoming master's IT program. This will allow me the opportunity to teach IT classes at UMGC. It would be like giving back to this awesome institution while guiding the next generation of future IT professionals through their journey.

Betty Graham

Betty Graham is a corporate facilities manager. A native of Florida, she recently moved to Nevada. With more than 35 years in the hospitality industry, she has held a variety of diverse positions. Now she is looking at a new future.

Honestly, as I look back on it all, I would tell my younger self, "you will be okay and survive," even though it would not have felt that way at the time. Sometimes we go through things in life that we would not wish on our worst adversary. I find that most motivating quotes, such as "everything we go through in life happens for a reason," do not take that aspect into account. So "no," some things happen that should never happen.

But I would also tell my younger self that you can and will succeed because you will come through the fire and be successful and happy on the other side. We may not like certain events in our life, but we can definitely learn from them. We are not successful in spite of what we have come through. We are successful because of our inner strength.

As I look back on it, the first 25 years of my life were made up of essentially two separate worlds lived in by one person. One of them was really horrible, which was the life that happened to me in my outer world. And the other was good and encouraging, but almost entirely internalized and intellectual, my inner world.

My "life in the outside" world was a perpetual struggle with my mother, my father, and our life as a family. When I was not quite seven, I was abused by a close family member. I was just supposed to deal with it. There was no parental intervention, no support, no mental health services. Nothing. Then it happened again by an even closer family member, because, well, the first one got away with it. By that time, at not yet nine years old, I had already determined that I couldn't trust anyone, so I kept it to myself. Survival was up to me. And that's the way it has been ever since.

My inner world was where I had better and more encouraging moments. It held me together through all of the trauma. All through the first 25 years, my internal life was very idea-oriented and intellectual. The one positive thing that mom did was to get us a lot of books and read to us. As a five-year-old, I read everything, including the boxes of cereal on the kitchen table. I read the little golden books, fairy tales, just devoured them. I read all the time. That continued into elementary school. The worse things got on the outside, the more I retreated further into books.

I was also super studious. I could escape into my classwork and find solace in whatever I was learning. At the same time, the inner me also became interested in music along with reading. From then on, reading and music became my go-to's and stress relievers. It was all internal, but that was how I dealt with life in order to keep my composure and manage for myself.

In middle school, I was in the top division academically and in band. I was also working in the reading lab, and I really loved that. All these things gave me positive reinforcement. In the eighth grade, I worked in the guidance counselor's office. This guy was wonderful. He cared about me as a person and talked about the future. And he encouraged me to think about college, the first time anyone had done that.

Thanks to that guidance counselor, I really started thinking about what I was capable of. In the ninth grade, I landed on languages as my goal. I started with French. I was really good at it, and I added Spanish to the mix the next year. At one point, I actually was thinking about going to a school In Paris and becoming an interpreter at the UN. The inner me was dreaming big.

All through these years, I was my own support. I figured out my own coping mechanisms. I was doing fine on the inside, but my outer life was not cooperating. So, I was doing summer school, working full-time, anything to not be at home. I wasn't thriving. I was just surviving and trying to hold my life together.

Shortly before my 18th birthday, it all fell apart. I stopped school and moved out on my own with a roommate. I knew I needed to finish high school to have any kind of life of my own design. It took three years, off and on, due to my emotional state and work, but I got my high school diploma. I knew I wanted to go on from there to college but was not ready to continue emotionally, financially, or in any other way.

Then, as they say, life happened. I had been told by doctors that pregnancy was not a viable option for me. But in 1991, one night with a friend changed that, and I was surprised to discover that I was pregnant with my first little miracle. But you know what? That little girl saved my life. After I had my daughter, I was living for someone else. So, I was taking care of myself and taking care of her at the same time.

This was a huge turning point for me, the first of several. I needed to think about someone else, and I wanted to set a good example. At first, I was working in hotels, at the front desk, and doing night audits. My mom would watch her when I was working at night. I never wanted her alone with my parents for all the obvious reasons. Then, I got a job as a sales associate at a retail store, and I loved it. Pretty quickly, they made me a manager. That was the first time someone else had actually recognized and rewarded me for being good at work. It was the beginning of my being tactical about getting ahead at work. I learned to show I could do the work and more. It was a small business, and I could move up without credentials. Soon, I was director of retail at three stores and managing a fourth store in tandem.

I was there for four years, but as my daughter approached school age, I thought I should get a more stable daily environment. So, I got an office job in a construction company with a little better pay and way better hours. That way, we could have a more set and regular schedule. She went to the before and after-school programs, and then I picked her up at the end of the day. We were together every night and weekends – a very consistent life.

Over the next five years, I worked my way up in several companies, moving around to take on improved opportunities. I stayed mostly in construction because I really liked the field. In the late '90s, I started doing more administrative assistant roles in the timeshare industry: expense reports, booking travel, contracts, and purchase orders. In one job, I ended up working with the senior VP for Acquisitions and Development. He recognized that I really had the ability and skills to support him very well. It was a huge boost to my self-image and sense of capacity. He was the first person since the guidance counselor in school to believe in my natural ability. He counted on me, and I learned a lot from him.

I was with him for six years. At the same time, I applied to a six sigma program and became a green belt. But I was turned down for higher positions because I didn't have a degree. I had the experience, but no degree. So, I knew I was always going to be compromised. As I look back on it all, I realized that without a degree, I was not getting any farther. I was repeatedly turned down for promotions in those larger companies because all I had was a high school diploma.

Then in 2002, after a short relationship, I learned I was pregnant with my second daughter. Now I had two kids to care for, send to college if they wanted, and give a good life. And my second little girl saved us all in that her arrival started me on a more serious path to working for our collective future.

I was 36 when she was born. In 2004, when she was just two, I started looking for schools and started a B.A. degree program. Then just as things were starting to settle a bit with school, work, and home, my mother had a stroke. All the years of psychosomatic behavior, manic depression, and diabetes finally took their toll. So now I was raising two children, working, trying to go to school, and caring for a sick mother. That was too much for me to handle. I stopped school in 2005 and began looking for a job that would use all of the valuable skills I had gained.

I found another development company, applied, and was hired into a coordinator position with a 25% raise. It was another step up. I was going to be more involved in acquiring property and land planning for resorts. I was fascinated with this work. It was a great company and a great experience. I learned a lot and got to do even more sophisticated work, including project management. But when a chance to advance came, I was not promoted because I was a single mother, if you can believe that!

On the one hand, there was nowhere in the company to go. But, on the other, I still needed and wanted to get the degree. So, I stayed put and went back to school a year later. But after a year into the program, I stopped again. Between working, mothering, dealing with my mother, and adding the financial factor, I felt like I had no options. During this time, I was also looking into other positions, still trying to move up. I finally left that position for another company, but then the economy crashed in 2008. First, my boss's position was eliminated, and then six weeks later, they let me go too.

And then things only got worse. I was looking for a job, but there weren't any to be had. Everything I had experience or knowledge in was in a serious downturn. After months of hoping and trying, my savings ran out, and we lost our apartment. We were well on our way to being homeless, and we moved into a one-room efficiency motel.

There was a moment during this terribly depressing and scary time that really opened my eyes. One day my younger daughter and I were at the motel's pool. It was a pretty filthy and awful pool, sort of like the motel itself. While we were there, I saw another mother looking blank-faced and hopeless, just staring off into the distance. No emotion, nothing. She clearly had accepted her situation and had stopped fighting. And, with a shock, I thought to myself, "at least I know this is only temporary for us." I knew that this was not long-term for my family. We would get out of this. I had my intelligence and resources, contacts, and skills. I went back to the motel room that night, determined to go back to school while we were there. And I started again trying to complete my degree while looking for work.

Eventually, I found a contract job at a hospitality construction company, right in my wheelhouse. I dug in and just started doing "my thing," using the collective effect of all my experience. I managed all sorts of things that were not on the list of my responsibilities. I was capable, I knew it, and they knew it. Even though I knew there was an end date to this job, I gave it my all and learned a lot in the process while still trying to make progress in my classes. In December 2010, the contract ended, and I stopped school again so that I could devote my resources to my family's needs.

But I knew I needed to further my education, and in 2011 I started another program again while unemployed. My oldest daughter was taking college courses toward her own degree, so it was very motivating to have two of us in the house working toward those goals. But while I wanted to continue, finances again got the better of me, and I had to stop once more. My girls came first, and they needed me to focus on keeping us afloat. With no job prospects, things were getting difficult again.

If I had had a degree, I would have had an employment identity. But with no degree, I had no relatable position identity, and most jobs were unavailable. So, I was a little random in the choices I had to make. For example, with unemployment about to run out, I took a job at a durable medical sales company from 2011 to 2013. I was back to making nothing, with no benefits, and I was increasingly miserable just trying to make ends meet. I was honestly at my wit's end and felt I could not withstand one more thing. So, I just stayed focused on the store while continuing to look for a better-paying job.

Thankfully, in 2013 my best friend was getting a promotion at work and called to see if I would be interested in applying for the job she was leaving. She thought

I would be a good fit. With that, I got back into the timeshare business with a good position as an executive assistant for the controller. Higher pay, benefits, great boss, all good. And I finally felt like I could breathe again.

This was the beginning of the next stage in my life, a transition, as I look back on it. After my first six months, my boss asked me where I wanted to be in 10 years. That was the first real support I had had in a long time. He understood my capacity and my interests and supported them. After a couple of years, there was a facilities manager opening, and I asked about it. I applied even though it required a B.A., I knew my experience was really germane. I got it because the boss didn't care about gender, race, or the degree. The question was simply could I do the job or not? The answer was "Yes." I finally got the promotion I had been waiting for after so many years in the business.

The next step was being transferred in the same role and a move to Nevada. When I got to the office in Las Vegas, I walked through the door with confidence. By now, my motto was "Make yourself the obvious choice. You never know what opportunities will come," thanks to the wise words of one of the senior leaders. If you don't open your mouth, people won't know what you know and what you are able to do.

And then along came the pandemic. Ironically, the pandemic gave me the time to collect my thoughts. I had been working extremely hard over the past couple of years, and a big turning point for me was a health scare I had after the pandemic began. It was not the virus, thank goodness, but it did give me the time to take a quiet look at my own mortality. Although I had provided for my daughters' physical needs, I had not been able to show them that they can move beyond surviving to success. Now I could do that. It was time to try again and prevail.

So, I began to focus on learning. I had an enormously wide range of experiences and "education," but they did not add up to one piece of paper. I needed the credential regardless of my experience and capabilities. I was looking at Purdue Global when I discovered their Open Degree Program. They would accept all the learning I had already done towards the degree. So, the degree program became a way to pull it all together on my own terms and time and at an affordable price. It was just what I needed. So, I enrolled in their Professional Studies Degree completion program for the B.A., and I only had to take 13 courses total to get my B.A.

But at the same time, other avenues were opening up for me. My career in hospitality and business had kind of fallen together as a matter of necessity. But now that my path forward was clearer, financially and emotionally, I wanted to do something more in line with my values.

Teaching English as a Second Language and Life Coaching have been interests of mine over the years. I have begun to think about having a bi-lingual approach to life coaching as a new direction in my professional life. I started taking some life coaching programs, and as I worked through the videos and exercises, I realized that I was also feeling a transformation in myself.

Looking ahead, I want to use my experiences to improve my ability to be a life coach. There are so many individuals who would benefit from the help in following their dreams and not taking the random path like I did. I feel there are better ways to help people to attain their goals than having them follow a prescribed program that has nothing to do with their interests. I think schools do a poor job of helping students figure out what drives them and what they really want to focus on in life. Too often, schools are just a clearing house to get as many students as possible onto the hamster wheel that requires everyone to have a job so they can buy things and get another job to buy more things and so on. There is nothing fulfilling in that path unless you are doing something that actually fills your soul and provides inner happiness.

We don't get to the end of our life thinking we should have made more money for someone else so that they could have their dream of having enough money. We get there regretting that we did not do things that mattered to us individually. The pandemic experience has given me the bridge to help people live happy, healthy creative, successful lives. That's what I want to do, follow my passion. No more hamster-like behavior and doing only what I have to do to survive.

Financial reality dictated that I do what I did. Now I want to help other people achieve their dreams by helping them learn English, coupled with life coaching on what they want to do with their future. Are they here to simply be a cog in the wheel of life? Or are they here to dream big and follow their own passion and values? I want to help them to do the latter.

I heard recently about a new college, College UnBound (CU). They use this method called the Core Project Rubric. The Project Rubric ensures that students are thinking ahead to what their communities need and how to be change leaders in the process. It also values past learning and skills, telling students the value of their knowledge and success. Also, students do not have to choose an elective course based on their major. Humans are far more complex than to have to engage in a particular set of courses because they are approved electives for the major being taken. And most often, the electives have nothing to do with the major anyway. It's totally arbitrary and illogical. Shouldn't an elective help you discover something about yourself and, in doing so, give you a more rounded education?

At the end of the day, we are social animals looking for connection and meaning. When modern society and education do not support that need, some people get lost because they elect life pathways and activities that are not positive solutions for their lives. The right kind of learning can not only help us find the right path, it can also help us understand that we have much more in common with each other than we may realize.

Section 4: The Capstone—Michael's Story

"Michael's Story" powerfully illustrates the two main points of *Stories form the Educational Underground*: the presence of enormous innate talent and intelligence just waiting to be recognized and encouraged and the power of personal learning. Michael shares his life journey and learning to date. His story illustrates how gaining opportunity in life was a journey that often contradicted powerful parts of his cultural background, history, and daily reality. And yet, drawing on his personal learning as well as formal education and great advice and support along the way, Michael persisted through thick and thin to a remarkable place of insight, knowledge, and understanding after 36 years.

Michael O'Bryan

I was born and raised in Hartford, Connecticut. I lived my first ten years in Hartford, right by the projects, with two older brothers and a single mom. She was an amazing woman, a survivor of foster care and human trafficking. And she wasn't going to let that happen to us.

I grew up poor but with a lot of love. In fact, I didn't realize we were poor until other kids made fun of me in elementary school. So, I didn't have cool sneakers, just "rejects." But, from the earliest days of my youth, my mom read and played music to me all the time. We would listen to music, read, and go to the library all the time. We didn't have a lot of money, but she invested a lot of time and love in me. She got her GED at 29, but she wanted her kids to be better educated than she had been so that we could be in a better place. She would say, "Make sure you see the world, Mike, make sure you travel and learn. Travel, but let companies pay for you to see the world." Learning has always been a fun endeavor to me, thanks to my mom.

All this reading and music as a youngster made a big difference. I could read, but I didn't know what was so special about knowing words as a five-year-old.

Here's a funny story. When I was 15, we were going to my aunt's church. One day we saw a woman who had been my early childhood teacher. When she saw me, she burst into tears. She told me that she was dyslexic and couldn't read very well when she was teaching me. She recalled that she had stumbled over a word when she was reading to the group. I came over and said, "I know that word," and then I read the whole sentence. That experience led her to get analyzed, find a solution, go to college, and move forward. She said, "You don't need anything more than to just be yourself."

Here's another story. In kindergarten, I was a good reader, and they wanted to reinforce that. These are very visceral and emotional memories because I would be getting ready to color, and then they would take me to read because I could read. I wanted to be with the colorers! Everyone else was playing with blocks or doing something in a circle, and I was over in the corner reading. I decided to pretend I couldn't read. That way, I could get the situation I wanted which was all three: reading and art and blocks.

By the time I was in second grade, I was reading two years ahead. But in fourth grade, they pulled me back because, due to all the moving around, I didn't have a home base in the school. My hairline is funny. I had reject shoes. I'm getting moved around in classes. Everyone, older kids and kids my age, was worked up about me, and things were not going well. Older kids were jealous because I could read so well. My classmates were jealous also, but for other reasons, like the girls wanted to read with me.

Copyright © by Michael O'Bryan. Reprinted by permission.

When I was 10, my brothers moved in with their father. That really was a shock, and I thought nothing would ever be the same. In a way, I was right because Mom and I moved to West Hartford, where I went to middle and high school.

Our new place was just down the road, but it might as well have been another world. It was as dramatically different as possible. In the beginning, I, literally and figuratively, kept my head down. I went from being in the vast majority of a school population of kids of color to being one of very few in a white kids' school. It was scary and really disorienting. These were the schools for the rich kids.

What a change it was. There were music classes, choir, a lot of other amazing resources. But I was having a hard time because I had gone from being in a class with no or one white kids to a room full of white kids with one or two Black kids. I was ten minutes away from where I had lived, but in a totally different environment. At first, I wanted to go back and definitely started acting out. One day I threw a chair at the window. They gave me an in-school suspension, but I was never dismissed. I think they were trying to figure out how to support me.

One day soon after that, I got called to lunch with my teacher to "get to know me better." I was reading *The Sword and the Stone* by T.H. White, and she was really interested in that. She introduced me to Ms. Fisher, the teacher who ran Quest, a gifted and talented program. And I was transferred into the program. It was amazing. I got to learn what I wanted, learn all kinds of things, go to interesting places, and meet interesting people from the big newspaper in Hartford.

In retrospect, I think they had my tests and knew I was capable. But I was acting out, and my teacher had figured that I had what it took on the scholastic end, but there was something wrong. And the gifted class was the solution. Was I lucky or what?

The next year I was in middle school. It was my first full year in school in West Hartford, and I ran for vice president of the student council. I won, and it was a great beginning to the year. Then I got a lead in the school musical. So, I was crossing into the art world as early as the sixth grade.

In eighth grade, it really moved to the next level when the Looking In Theatre came to school. Looking In Theatre is a theater group where kids did the acting using original content they'd created on significant issues – eating disorders, sex, LGBTQ, date rape, racism – all the issues that were difficult for teens. After they acted out the scenes, they held what they called a "talk back" in character with the audience, then did another set of scenes with another character-based "talk back." After that, the actors would break character and have a final "talk back" as themselves, discussing what it all meant and sharing relevant info on the subject matter covered with the audience.

It changed my life. I thought about being gay and closeted and about my family's trauma and its impact on me. And I started thinking about theater as a way to open up and communicate. But I kept it to myself. The next day at school, students were visiting guidance to discuss issues in their personal lives, and people were opening up to their teacher about issues in their lives. I was stunned. That was the impact of Looking In, of storytelling in the process of personal "meaning-making."

The next year I tried out for the group, got hired/accepted, and that was the beginning of it all. The creative process was incredible. They asked us to listen to people who actually had experienced or been impacted by the issues and scenarios we were acting out. What a learning experience that was. What a gift it was to learn from real people, families, and professionals dealing with human suffering, healing, and joy.

The next year, The Greater Hartford Academy of the Performing Arts (the performing arts magnet high school) accepted me, but there was no way I could afford it, and West Hartford High school wasn't going to pay. I was totally bummed. But the very next day, the head of the Theatre Department, who was also the director of Looking In Theatre, called and said that a donor had paid for a scholarship for me. I was thrilled and, frankly, in retrospect, a little taken aback. No one had ever done anything that financially significant for me before. I started the academy in the tenth grade, the beginning of the journey of my lifetime. I am still friends and in a relationship with a number of my teachers at the academy. Now they say, "you are the man we saw in the boy we worked with." That was, and still is, one of the most fulfilling comments or affirmations I've received in my adult life.

At varying points in my first and second year in the school, I was acting out, not preparing, all that kind of stuff. The teachers totally called me out on it. They said, "You keep this up and your scholarship is gone." So, from then on, I was all in. The summer in between my first and second year, a voice teacher said to me, "You have talent, but you don't believe in yourself." She gave me voice lessons all summer, and it really helped me understand my talent a bit more. And that was important because there was still a lot of stuff going on at home. One of my brothers was going through a lot and left home again early in my sophomore year, and mom was working all the time to support us. So, I had to really focus and try to pull up.

Meanwhile, I wasn't doing anything to succeed at my regular high school. I was in a 50/50 program between the high school and the arts academy. I missed more than 50 days my 10th-grade year because I just didn't care, and I was performing a lot during the day for pay. So, I had legit excuses and often used those opportunities to blur the lines with my desire to just not be in a school. I was all into the arts and decided to put more energy into the arts academy. And since my mother worked the third shift in a group home and pulled other shifts as well, I was at home alone a bunch. I was sort of doing my own thing in the morning and then going to the Arts school in the afternoon.

And then, thank God, I got caught. Mom asked me how I was doing at high school one day. I lied about being there, and she called me flat out because I was skipping, and she knew it. I remember thinking that I had really let her down, but she appeared to leave it alone.

The next day I got up, and she was there. She took me to school and came in with me. It was November 2001, my Junior year in school, and we met with all my teachers. It was an ambush: my teachers, my guidance counselor, head of guidance, both vice-principals. In retrospect, it was one of the most loving acts I've ever experienced, and I remember it to this day. They told me that I would not graduate on time if I missed any more school. They said, "You are too smart for this." They understood that if my mom pulled me out of the Arts Academy, it would destroy me. So, they wanted me to just try harder and advocated for me to stay. It was a form of privilege to me, a type of intellectual privilege, if you will. So, they gave me the benefit of the doubt. And I responded sufficiently.

Later that year, I did two songs in a showcase performance event and had leads in a number of plays and musicals. I did professional theatre and voiceover work for pay all during high school. A world had emerged for me, and I grabbed the whole thing like a bull by the horns during the 11th and 12th grades. It was a unique experience all the way through.

By the time I was a senior, I was cooking. And when I wanted to go to college, I got into the University of the Arts in Philadelphia, and that met a major criterion. I wanted to go to Philly and be Black on stage and in life, not in a special role. For all the great things that had happened for me in West Hartford, there was a lot of "normative canon" casting there. I wanted authentic and varied Black roles and experiences.

At UArts, I had terrific Black teachers. Though there were only a few, they were into the arts in a way I wouldn't have gotten elsewhere. There were racial issues there, but I had teachers who protected me.

I finished school in four years, but I had a bumpy start. I failed my first semester piano course, and my mom said, "do that again and I'll get you back to the community college." I said to myself, "no way," and took some private lessons to catch up.

I also took courses that truly changed my understanding of life and music. Courses that helped me develop an understanding of art and music through the lens of cultural anthropology and ethnomusicology. I took another amazing class called "Perceptions" that tied neuroscience to psychology, sense-making of stimuli reception, and general emotional understanding.

A huge chunk of UArts was me journeying to find myself. Much of my high school experience was atypical. I had all these opportunities that I maxed out on. But I didn't know that they were special; to me, that was normal. I was taking classes called "Theatre and Social Action" in high school and learning about theatre of the oppressed and arts-based liberation movements in other parts of the world. But I swallowed a lot of those interests to try and make friends or to stay close to my friends during college. I had this burning thing on the inside that I was trying to figure out – what does it all mean?

Then a strange and wonderful thing happened. I met a man experiencing homelessness named Mr. James. Mr. James was a fantastic soul and one of the most caring human beings I've ever had the pleasure of experiencing. That relationship and our conversations over the next several years opened me to a lot of new perceptions. The experience of meeting him changed my life. Mr. James was a remarkably wise man who had a lot of life challenges. He called me "young man," even though I told him my name, and his wisdom was bittersweet; the kind of wisdom that is rooted in reminiscing that itself was rooted in regret. When we talked, he used his state in life to speak to me about my life. How do you use your life energy and the things that life presented you to move forward? I learned a lot from what he wished he could go back and reimagine. That kind of thing.

We met because I was a night bird, and one night, after I was done writing music, I was walking around at 1:30 am. I went to 7/11, and there he was, and he asked me for water. I asked him, "How do you get water if no one gives it to you"? And he replied, "puddles if need be," and that blew my mind. I had never imagined something like that. His was a cruel life, but he was very kind, and we made a habit of meeting every now and then. The last time I saw him, I was 25, and I hadn't seen him in more than a year. I went downtown, and I had actually been looking for him for some weeks at that time.

That day, I was walking with a friend and randomly decided to take a turn I actually didn't mean to make. All of a sudden, I heard "Young man!" and there he was. Had I turned one block earlier or later, I would never have seen him. He began immediately telling me that he had hope because of people like me, and he began crying and sharing that he had prayed for me to walk by because I always shared food with him and reminded him of his own dignity of being. I got him the food he wanted, hugged him, and that was the last time I saw him. I will always remember that moment, as he kept comparing my heart to the callousness of many people's hearts and lovingly yelling at me to keep it that way. The world can be such a cold and cruel place, but I will never forget the lessons and things that Mr. James taught me.

Then I met the "real" real world. I graduated and got a job in Miami working with LatinX migrant farmworkers. We lived in Miami and got bussed 25 miles out into the countryside to meet them. It was a whole new experience. They lived in brutal poverty, low wages, no running water in the house, afraid of the law, all of it. I had grown up poor, but this was beyond the pale. That was it. It was the moment and the turning point when I determined that I would use art to address trauma and reimagine a world that would be more equitable and just than the one my peers and I had inherited. We could redesign the future that was already designed for us. I went back to Philly to make it happen. I knew I couldn't go back to working in a movie theater. I ended up working in emergency housing, worked as an after-school arts teacher, and then they gave me a job.

Working there, at The Red Shield Family Residence, is where I really took a deep dive into understanding trauma and chronic stress and its impact on individuals, relationships, and systems. Using that information, I was able to build culturally responsive arts programs for youth and young adults that helped them develop supportive relationships with other adults and to also use art to help address trauma and strengthen their psychosocial development.

Working with a mentor, Susan Brotherton (who I lovingly call my social work mom), I began presenting my work and methods to varying professionals both inside and outside of the clinic world. I eventually moved into representing the Red Shield in city-wide policy advocacy as it related to youth and young adults experiencing homelessness. While simultaneously doing that, I was music directing and teaching at The New Freedom Theatre, writing original teen musicals with youth from across the city of Philadelphia addressing issues that impacted youth and young adults. It was really a full-circle moment for me, given the experiences and training that I had growing up.

By this time, I was invited to join a city-wide project called Journey2Home, where a collection of lead artists spent a year working with youth impacted by the issue of housing insecurity. Journey2Home was a fantastic experience for me both as a human being and as a professional working at the intersection of art and public health. At the same time that I was working on Journey2home, I was also working on the city of Philadelphia's first youth "point in time" count. The "point in time" count is the federal government's main methodology used to identify folks experiencing homelessness. And for the first time, the government was requiring cities that receive federal funds to address the issue of homelessness to count young people experiencing homelessness between the ages of 18 and 26. And so at this point in my career, I was really beginning to see that my approach to art and justice and storytelling, my ways of developing understanding and a sense of knowing, and my commitment to the issues were being recognized in different sectors, even though I was still a novice and not necessarily the best at what I was doing. I appreciated that people saw some sparks of leadership in me and thought my energy could support or help make some things happen.

Soon after that, I shifted roles. I left The Red Shield Family Residence and ended up as a contractor at the US Attorney's Office of Eastern Pennsylvania in collaboration with The Sanctuary Institute. The Sanctuary Institute houses a model called The

Sanctuary Model created by a woman who has become a dear friend and mentor of mine named Dr. Sandra Bloom, along with two of her colleagues, Joseph Foderaro and Ruth Ann Ryan. Sanctuary is an organizational cultural model that was designed to teach an organization's staff, from the top tier of leadership down to frontline workers, what it means to be trauma-informed and focused on understanding that, in the words of the model's creators, it's never about what's wrong with a person, but instead it is all about what's happened to them. The model works on the premise that everyone is coming to any given moment or experience with accumulated histories and prior experiences that have shaped their mental models, behaviors, and expectation management. It also shapes how a person will maneuver the world and how they believe the world works and responds to them.

I'd spent years in training and working with this model at the Red Shield Family Residence. Over that time, I was also diving deeper into the study of critical race theory, design principle, behavioral economics, and the science of resilience. I wanted to complement what I was learning about trauma with a wider view of systems as it relates to the ways in which humans gave organized social geography and identity into policy, access, and resource allocation. And I'm glad I did all of that because my job with The US Attorney's Office was to really think about how we can use public health frameworks and the theory behind trauma and chronic stress to address issues of youth homicide and adult recidivism in North Philadelphia. That was such a learning process for me because I understood the community context, but I didn't understand how bureaucratic systems fully worked. I had some experience dealing with them, but not in this manner. While working on this, I also ended up getting employment at the Village of Arts and Humanities, where I'm now their Director of Learning. When I came to the village, I was mainly tasked with designing and running the afterschool and summer programming for youth ages 9 to 19, which was already a pretty intense job with a lot of staff to supervise. Over time, my role grew to include managing special community-wide projects, developing new programming that now allows us to provide paid opportunities for youth up to the age of 26, and an employer-focused professional learning community centered on Diversity Equity and Inclusion and Racial Equity and Inclusion. I think one of the things that's become clear to me through all of this work was that so much of it challenged what I knew and what I thought I knew. It also reaffirmed what I did know and what I thought I didn't know.

And I am very much the man I am today because of many of the trials and errors that I have been through. You know, hindsight is always 2020. And luckily, failure is only an occurrence that truly takes place when you stop trying, have not gained any skills and insight, or have not learned how to create healthy relationships moving forward. It's human to go through a period where the outcomes might not be what you desired, or you do not achieve everything you set out to do, and so you feel like you failed. I've tried to make sure that I learn as much as I can from those situations and pay it forward for myself and others by extending grace and compassion for the fully human frailties that accompany all of our greatness.

Humans are walking contradictions, paradoxes, and tensions in opposition…and there's something complex, beautiful, and amazing in that if we can learn to harness those moments and allow them to act as fertile ground for growth and change. And so, all of those experiences helped me get to really to where I am today. I now have my own strategic design and have worked with regional and national clients in the for-profit and not-for-profit sector and am continuing to really challenge myself on what I think I know while creating more opportunities and space for the voices and experiences of others to be shared, heard, and centralized. And that's not just on projects or work but in the context of how we understand their humanity and, by default, our collective humanity.

I've been fortunate to travel the world, never paying for it really. And, you know, I feel like I've fulfilled that dream or that piece of advice my mother gave me in childhood which was to learn and travel the world on companies' expenses. She'd always say let them pay for you to come and talk and think, let them pay for that brain. And I've been able to do that.

It's been wild to think back to being this poor little kid who grew up with a ton of love and grew up with the opportunity to invest in himself and who was fortunate enough to have people invest in him and hold him up. You know, when I gave up on myself, there were people there to hold me up when I had bottomed out because of life stress and trauma. There were people there to pick me up and hold me up. And a lot of people don't have that. So, I'm eternally grateful. I've been able to speak on stages nationally and internationally and at conferences and organizations that range from public health and trauma, design, city planning, art education, community economic development, creative placemaking, developmental science, neighborhood development, healthcare, and more! I mean, I have truly been fortunate and am so grateful. My goal now is to continue to grow as a person but to also grow my firm and assist people, organizations, and institutions that are trying to understand the mechanics of our humanity and how they can center humanity in all of their operations, internally and externally.

The core of my work is the belief that cultivating a new shared view of humanity is the way forward and that the work of the 21st century is to address the roots of culture that are steeped in dehumanization as the default operating system and design principle for policymaking and culture building. We have to understand that dehumanization is at the core of the growth of the Western world and, in particular, the American Journey and narrative. From there, we can begin to name and explore how dehumanization (racism, sexism, ableism, xenophobia, homophobia, transphobia, classism, etc.) has shaped our modern world and mental models and begin the process of "rehumanizing" ourselves.

That rehumanizing effort is the work of defining and then implementing shared frameworks of our full humanity that sees us all in the beauty of our diversity, as being part and parcel to one another's well-being, and one another's positive evolution. I think it's time that we consciously evolve. And I learned all that years ago through the power of art to help teenagers consciously evolve, let alone all the other things that I saw art and meaning-making do for people and groups through my work and travel. So yeah. I think the opportunities are boundless, and they are humanity's for the taking. This is what I learned outside of college and in the university of life, love, and humanity.

Through it all, high school and college gave me the opportunity to fall in love with theater and the arts and to grow up a little. But there was powerful learning outside of school during and after my formal education.

Theater exposed me to so much. My obsession with art is really about storytelling and the lived embodiment of human experience. Music was an avenue and a very lucky gifting for me, as was writing and theater. I have been working with all three to better understand the human condition.

During college, my love for developmental science and neuroscience really emerged. I immersed myself in science, anthropology, psychology, and more and did that inside and outside of school. That exploration continued well after college and still exists to this day. Traveling through these disciplines was like finding breadcrumbs that were leading me along a path.

I had to be careful to not allow people to push me into dichotomizing or splicing myself while taking this journey; life, employers, and the status quo have a way of doing that. College was a place where I could explore. But the work world and our "normative" society were a big problem. What I know now is that my global and macro way of thinking seemed confusing and disjointed to some of my employers, colleagues, and others in my life. Sometimes people would comment about me seemingly having ADD/ADHD.

I am very curious and always have been. I just have a natural sense of curiosity. As a child, I never got discouraged from asking questions. My aunt Barbara helped raise me and always said to me that, "the only dumb question is the question never asked." So, with that affirmation, I've always moved through life empowered to ask questions. I brought that with me to school, to art, to life. I am always looking for the next question because I've learned that what one knows or thinks they know, they probably do not know completely. And that is human. You have to ask new questions, learn more, and continually reorganize your understanding of yourself and the knowledge and experiences you've accumulated over the years.

Epistemology is all about questioning and probing what knowledge is; how do we know what we know? Who gets to say what knowledge is and to determine which data confirms what knowledge. And that's only part of the story. Long before we had our contemporary forms of data, stories were the way we communicated big ideas, knowledge, and history. I am not against data science, but that is only one piece or part of the "knowing circle," not the whole thing. Story and narrative also belong in that circle as well, especially when we are trying to invest in human beings. Humans are creatures of meaning and accumulated meaning over time; we are always making or trying to make meaning out of the world around us and our place in it. Being curious about the experience of others and collecting varying forms of data [including story and the person's perceived meaning(s)] are crucial to my work.

So, what is the connection between epistemology and curiosity? Babies "know" nothing. But they are naturally curious. It's part of the process by which they learn to stand, to walk, to run, to talk. They also learn "who" they are through this curiosity and the network of relationships available to them. This early method of discovery/knowing doesn't leave us as we age. We just supplant its dominant role in our lives with the scholastic experience. This tension is not named for students when we enter school, so we need to reinforce and encourage curiosity in a country where school typically doesn't encourage or support that across the developmental span. That is why the arts are a great space for little kids as well as older people. Creative learning environments provide the kind of scaffolding for the human experience that allows us to activate and direct the power of curiosity. In those environments, we use varying modalities and methods to practice inquiry, analysis, synthetization, and dissemination.

The Neuroscience of Emotions (Adolphs and Anderson, 2018) speaks to an aspect of this issue and offers a way for us to organize and understand emotional experiences. Adolphs and Anderson are working on the notion that when we use the term emotion, we are combining physiology, behavior, and the meaning made out of the moment. They suggest that those three ingredients combine to define an emotional experience.

So, by default, "meaning-making" is a crucial process and tool in developing emotional intelligence and also how we come to know what we know. Art opens the opportunity for people to participate in the space of "meaning-making" in ways that can support intentional growth and development. So, artmaking and other methods of making meaning, already exist but we are not organizing and using it to our advantage as a species. In fact, I have been struggling and working to metabolize all of this inside myself – challenging my ways of being and seeing in the world. They were inchoate before, and now I am trying to make them explicit. I had the instinct, and now I have learned how to use and harness it.

Conclusion

These stories speak for themselves. They reveal a combination of intelligence, talent, and perseverance, coupled with powerful learning and reflection driven by life's experiences. And, as many of the people interviewed reflected to me during our conversations, the opportunity to experience, first-hand, the validation of their personal learning by others, to get economic and academic value for it, was truly empowering.

In closing, I have to admit that the process of speaking with these people and organizing their stories has been a significant learning journey for me in and of itself. I have been pulled into a new space.

Prior to this effort, I had 50 years of experience in higher education, working largely with innovative models for low-access adults and lifelong learners. I had also written four books about adult learners, innovative practices and models, and the need for higher education to respond to a changing world. For example, my most recent book was *Free-Range Learning in the Digital World, The Coming Revolution in College, Career, and Education* (2018).

But then the COVID-19 pandemic hit and brought the multiple insecurities of millions of Americans to the surface in a very public and excruciating fashion. While I had been deeply aware, both intellectually and philosophically, of marginalized people's multiple insecurities, the impact of COVID-19 brought it home humanly. It forced me to rethink and deepen my understanding of the consequences of economic insecurity in America and its impact on people's lives, including education, housing, and health. And I began to think of education for learning and work as more than an access issue. It became, in my mind, a social justice issue as well.

That is why I wanted to "get beyond the data" and share the stories of people who are born on the far side of the opportunity gap. Having met the people in my book and listened to their stories, however, I was challenged to go even deeper. Education and work are integral parts of a larger American mosaic. And all the lines in this mosaic converge and reinforce a larger picture of societal health. Consequently, I found myself forced to re-think the responsibilities of a democratic government, the concepts of liberty and justice, the consequences of denying equal opportunity in education and work, and why achieving it is an urgent necessity.

With that in mind, I'll repeat what I said in the Introduction. The people you met in this book are success stories. But they are exceptions. They are the heroes in a sad saga where millions of other people are unable to navigate the pathway to opportunity. Ironically, these heroes could be portrayed as icons of the traditional American Dream, and in a sense, they are. Yes, these folks worked hard and overcame tremendous obstacles on their way to personal success. And that personal success, as many of them attested, will spill over and create opportunity for others. But as a society, we need these stories to become mainstream reality, not exceptions to the rules. And we need these "stories from the underground" to become part of the public consciousness when it comes to respecting and validating personal learning and work experience.

We cannot afford to discourage millions more success stories like these ones. The final phrase in our Pledge of Allegiance – With Liberty and Justice for All - suggests the heart of the American promise. Clearly, our progress towards meeting this commitment has been uneven, to say the least. There has been an ongoing ebb and flow throughout our history that has pitted the more "individual" notion of Liberty against the more "societal" notion of justice for all. And the question remains, can you have equal parts liberty and justice for all?

Liberty suggests individualism, that people have the right to act freely and as they see fit. But there are limits to that freedom. When Patrick Henry said, "Give me liberty or give me death," he was demanding representative government and freedom from the tyranny of the English Monarchy, not the right to do whatever he wanted, whenever he wanted.

On the other hand, justice, while protecting the individual, is inclusive, stretching across the multiple differences among us. Justice asserts equal treatment before the law and a seat at the table of opportunity that America promises for everyone.

I believe that, as we move beyond this pandemic and into the future, the arc of history in America is bending towards "justice for all." It calls us to provide fair treatment for all before the law while increasing security for all in the critical areas of income, health, housing, and education.

Liberty allows me to live my life as I choose, within the laws as passed and enforced by a representative government. It is, if you will, the "warp" of the fabric of democracy. Justice, on the other hand, is the "woof" of that fabric. It champions society's larger responsibility to treat all people fairly before the law and to provide for their basic needs. Together, balanced appropriately given the needs of people and the times, they create a coherent and stable environment for the people.

I have the right to live securely and enjoy the benefits of good health, a good education, a good job, and economic security. But, even as I support the tenets of liberty and individual rights, can I not also support justice, giving others access to essential levels of security and opportunity in these critical areas?

The COVID-19 pandemic has ripped back the curtain of denial to expose two harsh truths. First, it has revealed the reality of the grievous increase in income inequality since 1980. The people most affected are front-line workers and the poor of all ages and races. A wealth chasm exists between many of those most affected by the virus and the more affluent among us. And it is supported by systemic discrimination.

Second, we have taken these people for granted, benefitting from their labor while largely ignoring their contributions and the sources of their despair. They were with us long before the pandemic struck. Now we must pay attention to their needs. Because the costs of not doing so, lost opportunity and hope, illness, and economic insecurity, will ultimately compromise and weaken our country as they undermine our trust in government and each other. As Abraham Lincoln said at another critical turning point in American history, "A house divided against itself cannot stand."

Some might ask, however, "can this understanding of justice be overdone? Shouldn't people take responsibility for their own lives and self-improvement?" Of course, the answer is "yes." And, as I wrote earlier, effort matters. But let's dig a little deeper.

One of the pillars of American mythology is the "bootstrap" theory of self-improvement and personal progress. In this thinking, the individuals pull themselves to a better station in life by their own bootstraps, i.e., personal initiative and drive. And even though we know that self-levitation is not possible, we have let this anti-gravity metaphor dominate our thinking about where responsibility lies for getting ahead and improving your lot in American society. We all can agree that effort matters. In the continuing tension between Liberty and Justice, however, I believe the time has come to say that personal progress is not the sole responsibility of the individual. Other factors matter a lot.

Even in colleges where commitment to access and success are core to the mission, the "bootstrap fallacy" is alive and well. In fact, it permeates our language, our assumptions about learners and learning, and our practices. And for "just" practices to join "best" practices in learning and work, this must change.

Our language. When you go to a hospital, you are looking for a solution to a health problem that you have. And the focus is on care and recovery whenever possible. All the language points in that direction. When you go to college, however, success is positioned as a challenge. If you meet the challenge and pass, we say that you have persisted. Persistence defines learning as a struggle, a burden the learner must bear successfully to get ahead.

Persistence has largely been treated as the responsibility of the learner, not a shared responsibility with others. When one fails to complete a degree or a certificate, the traditional judgment has been that s/he either lacked sufficient intelligence, stick-to-it-iveness, or was simply not up to the challenge. The fault, the lack, lay with them. The life stories you read earlier, however, tell a very different story. They illustrate that life circumstances and life itself, not individual capacity, can and often do block the path to opportunity.

Our assumptions. Similarly, the substance of what is taught, and its structure, is generally determined by others and applied to the learner regardless of the learner's needs. So, an English as a Second Language course might be considered non-credit, and its successful completion a requirement for beginning "real" college. But a course in Spanish or French would count for academic credit. Since when is it less valuable to know English than French? And if you learn Mandarin while incarcerated, is that less valuable as a consequence? And how many low-income learners do we lose because they cannot access financial aid for non-credit courses? Or, in the workplace, should the life experience and prior learning brought by someone from a different life path, culture or socio-economic status be devalued and ignored because it isn't on a transcript or the "certification" is from a non-collegiate source?

The Bootstrap Fallacy asserts that not only must you self-levitate successfully, but that you also must do so by others' rules and expectations, others' assumptions about what a quality academic experience is and how much learning is enough. And so, as you read, time after time, legitimate and applicable learning done elsewhere – another college, a non-collegiate program, or experientially - is not accepted by many colleges. This costs adult learners time and money, and as one person told me, "It's like buying the same train ticket twice."

Our practices. And, historically, you had to do it alone, without counseling or other support, including good information about what you are studying and why. In the new ecosystem, those services and supports like these will be integrated with the curriculum and learner experience. This integration and personal support begin to make the learning journey a team effort, a shared responsibility, instead of a solo experience.

Nordstrom's gives you concierge service as a shopper; they do it because they have learned that people buy more and return to the store more often if they are assisted. An education and work concierge service supports learners in their primary endeavor – learning - while removing obstacles and responding to needs that might frustrate learning along the way. The odds are that, with this support, they will learn more and succeed more quickly.

Finally, another example. We know that beginning learners are the most vulnerable and prone to failure. Why, then, do we too often place them in large classes while graduate students, already proven successful learners, get small group and 1:1 treatment? If an emergency room behaved this way, they would make the sickest people wait while they served those who were healthier.

Practices in the new ecosystem will begin with a deep respect for and understanding of the needs of the learners, including life circumstances, personal history, and aspirations. We need to evaluate policies and practices to determine whether they are "learner-friendly." And we need to create support and engagement structures which free the learner to do the learning and which come to the learner's aid when life intervenes to frustrate the ability to learn.

Most of these success stories from the educational underground have a consistent narrative in one important sense. As the stories described in Sections Three and Four, often there was someone there to help at a critical time, a mentor or an advisor. And there was a new pathway available, either within a business, a new type of college, or a new service being offered that provided the right support at the right time to propel someone on the way to opportunity.

We are moving away from the era when providers of educational services called all the shots, set the standards, and declared winners and losers. And we are moving into a time when responding to the needs of the learner in every respect will be the core value of this ecosystem. This means that learners and employers will be sharing the driver's seat with colleges, helping to call the shots on everything, including quality assurance. Because if the learners get what they came for—satisfaction, a better job, a new avocational interest—that is the definition of quality. And if the employer onboards or upskills an employee who can do their job very well on day one, that is the definition of quality. In this world, college is not something to be "done." Learning and education is a lifelong pursuit, informed by a GPS for learning and work, that gives the learner knowledge, skills, and abilities with which to better navigate their lives in happy and productive ways.

More generally, as a nation and as individuals, we need to become more reflective about our lives, learning from our experiences more completely and making a deeper meaning from them as a result. I believe that reflection is the process of extracting meaning from experience. As we reflect, we understand more fully what any given experience—whether it is reading an Emily Dickenson poem, overcoming failure at work, or a turning point in our personal lives—has meant to us, how it has enriched us and given us new perspective. Consider T.S. Eliot's description of learning, reflection, and re-discovery along life's journey in his epic poem, Little Gidding (1934).

> We shall not cease from exploration
> And the end of all our exploring
> Will be to arrive where we started
> And know the place for the first time.

Eliot is telling us to be open to the lessons of life and the understandings which they create.

And finally, through advocacy and new government policies, such as means-tested lifelong learning student aid and corporate tax incentives for learning opportunities, we must bring the practices which made these heroes' stories possible from the educational underground to the surface. We need to bring personal learning from the margins to the mainstream of American life for the good of all. Until the personal learning of all people is respected and acknowledged, the systemic discrimination that exists in America today will continue to prevail. And the American promise is greater than that.

Personal Learning is more than just a nice phrase. It feeds us every day as we grow and change and adapt to the unfolding narrative of our lives. Let us live as Alberto Rios (2020) wrote in "A House Called Tomorrow,"

> *Look back only for as long as you must,*
> *Then go forward into the history you will make.*

Excerpt from "Little Gidding" from *Four Quartets* by T.S. Eliot. Copyright © 1942 by T.S. Eliot, renewed 1970 by Esme Valerie Eliot. Reprinted by permission of Houghton Mifflin Harcourt Publishing Company. All rights reserved.

Alberto Rios, excerpt from "A House Called Tomorrow" from *Not Go Away is My Name*. Copyright © 2018, 2020 by Alberto Rios. Reprinted with permission of The Permissions Company, LLC on behalf of Copper Canyon Press, coppercanyonpress.org.

Afterword

By Louis Soares
Chief Learning and Innovation Officer
American Council on Education

Rashaan Green, Sarah Aronack, Michele Daniels, Rashim Fazal, Anna Raymond.... if we continued telling more personal learning stories, we would quickly arrive at 71 million—the number of working-age Americans with no post-secondary credential, according to the US Census Bureau. Connecting the richness of the human capital embodied in these individuals in thoughtful and appropriate ways to formal post-secondary education and credentials may hold the keys to inclusive economic growth and a just and resilient democracy.

Stories from the Education Underground provides us with an intimate look inside the undervalued and underused human capital of millions of Americans. The very intimacy is a useful reminder that though the nation may have education challenges at scale, learning remains a remarkably human and personal endeavor. The art and science of aligning this most human of activities with formal education for scaled societal benefit is the attempt in the reflection that follows.

Art and science form an appropriate continuum for the possible processes needed to transform the substance of one thing, informal, personal learning, into the substance of another, a formal and structured, college education/credentials. We will need to draw on the inspiration and creativity associated with art as well as the data and experimentation associated with science to align these two different forms of learning. We can see this continuum alive in the emergent data we glean from the neuroscience of learning and student engagement with digital tools and the creativity manifest in the diverse variety of alternative learning pathway experiments that seemingly grow every day. Merging art and science, we may yet create an ecosystem of post-secondary education that enables all human potential for individual and societal benefit. Such an ecosystem would be self-sustaining and would systematically, adaptably, and resiliently connect all learning. It remains an aspiration, but as the stories in this text poignantly reveal, we cannot afford to fail to pursue it.

The post-secondary education ecosystem is comprised of many stakeholders that play both a role in and benefit from the growth of individual human capital including colleges and universities, K-12 schools, public libraries, employers, federal, state, and local governments, community-based organizations, neighborhood associations, and families. As we consider the diversity of interests, motivations, and resources each stakeholder brings to the

Copyright © by Louis Soares. Reprinted by permission.

personal learning journeys of millions of individuals, a short primer on ecosystems can help to understand what success looks like. Formally, an ecosystem is a biological community of interdependent organisms and the physical environment. Less formally, it is a complex network or interconnected system of people, organizations and/or other entities. Critical to the adaptation of the term ecosystem in non-biologic settings, including that of education, is the preservation of the meaning of interdependence. Interdependent organisms are those that are dependent on each other for life. If they are not interacting with and feeding each other's processes, they die and the ecosystem collapses. As we extend the ecosystem analogy to education stakeholders, we must always ensure that colleges, employers, community-based organizations, etc. are truly interdependent. Otherwise, the ecosystem framing does more harm than good because it creates false expectations about mutuality and resultant actions. Perhaps the most important interdependence in the post-secondary education ecosystem is the ability to document, validate and share learning and its outcomes across stakeholder settings. Without processes that serve this function, no ecosystem can flourish. A historical example of this ability is the process of awarding credit for prior learning for workplace training. This process transforms knowledge useful in a workplace into college credits that form the foundation of a degree pathway. As performed by my employer, the American Council on Education, this involves a structured review of workplace training by college faculty experts in the given discipline. In its current form, this ability has existed and evolved over a 60-year period. It is important to note that it remains a heavily human activity and thus, in its current form, has scale limitations that are not consonant with ecosystem sustainability and growth.

More contemporaneous examples of processes and tools that can support ecosystem sustainability include blockchain technologies that document and share verified learning across stakeholder groups and competency-based education, which develops conventions and standards for defining knowledge, skills and abilities in ways that transcend stakeholder silos thus creating a flow of learning. Both of these approaches enable and sustain the true interdependence necessary for an ecosystem to form and sustain itself.

The art and science to enable this ecosystem must be enacted, first and foremost, by a deep reverence for personal learning. Personal learning cannot be separated from the needs and aspirations of individuals. Its simple existence does not automatically make it the stuff of linear pathways to formalized college programs and credentials. An anecdotal example of why reverence for the individual is key, drawn from the experience of credit for prior learning work, is that many military service members pursue college credentials in disciplines far from domains in which they received workplace training. This makes connecting their personal learning derived from military service to college credentials a non-linear and, perhaps, ecosystem-stretching endeavor. For an ecosystem to form, the needs and aspirations of individuals and their personal learning must be the always and imminent catalyst.

To explore the contours of the ecosystem, we must first revisit the author's definition of personal learning. Then the exploration must elaborate on two key stakeholders in the ecosystem - the formal post-secondary education and employer communities. With regard to colleges and universities, we look into the paradox of diversity and homogeneity in the US higher education system with a revelatory corollary into the early history of adult learning. Employers are viewed through the scale of investment in learning and incentives for lasting engagement. With these observations in place, guiding themes for understanding and building an ecosystem that connects personal learning and the post-secondary education system are elaborated. The Afterword closes with a reflection on the opportunity and risks of not creating the ecosystem.

The research demonstrates that personal learning is an internal, contextual, nuanced, iterative, and organic process. This process plays out across the domains of human lives—political, economic, social, and spiritual—as indicated by the breadth of stakeholders that help build human potential in the ecosystem. Interestingly, as this text reveals, the intersection of process and context creates and recreates over a lifetime who an individual is as a citizen, caregiver and worker or entrepreneur. With this framing, we recall from the Introduction the definition that Personal Learning....*is all that other learning that you do, learning that is not planned by schools and colleges. It includes learning:*

- *From your culture and personal traditions*
- *On the job, at home, and in the community*
- *With colleagues, supervisors, family, neighbors, and friends*
- *Directly from life experiences, as well as via the computer, the library, or other data and information sources.*

Any ecosystem approach to connecting personal learning and post-secondary education and credentials must be deeply present to the experiences, locales, people, and resources that are the raw material of personal learning. From this raw material is born the pre-existing knowledge, intrinsic motivation to learn, and the first identity of the adult as a learner. These elements are the foundation of the art and science that successfully brings the personal learner into an ally relationship with formal post-secondary education.

This foundation will require all stakeholders in the ecosystem to change their practices for seeing and documenting what individuals know and are able to do. For colleges, it means transformative change in marketing, selection, and enrollment practices that reflect the connection between what is already learned and what learning is to come. For businesses, it means a form of skills-based hiring and talent development, aligned to personal learning, that is employee-driven and firm agnostic such that an individual can change jobs and, even employers, and continue a learning journey that builds human capital. For both businesses and colleges, it means relinquishing exclusive control of records of learning so that they can flow with the individual across all stakeholders as their personal learning journeys transcend boundaries. K-12 and other community stakeholders in the ecosystem will face similar transformational change. The key is to allow the foundations of personal learning to guide purposeful transformation even when it feels difficult, even counterintuitive.

With the foundations of personal learning as a foundation and guide, this reflection now turns to two key stakeholders – post-secondary education institutions and employers.

The US higher education system is paradoxically both diverse and homogeneous. Diverse in the sense that there are two- and four-year degree-granting institutions (approx. 4,200) along with a variety of institutions (approx. 2,000) offering other post-secondary credentials. This raw number is inclusive of varying missions, geographic catchment, religious and social imperatives. An additional element of diversity is in the range of credentials offered via colleges and universities, ranging from short-term certificates to doctoral degrees. (Although the pedagogical connection across this breadth of offerings is tenuous in the extreme.)

The system is homogenous in two ways. First, there is a practical homogeneity driven by regulatory and quality assurance constraints. The dominant regulatory regime, federal and state policy, a quality assurance approach, and regional accreditation, frame an academic, finance, and governance model that limits substantive innovation driven by material differences in student/customer needs. The needs of the working-age population, as described in the learning journeys in this book, constitute such a material difference. Second, as already noted in this text, from the mid-twentieth century until now, America has embraced a mental model of college framed by the image of an 18 to 24 year-old being dropped off at a residential, four four-year campus while financially dependent on their parents. This mental model, however unsupported by the data, holds great sway over what we as a society are willing to view as legitimate learning and quality education. Consequently, our default models for documenting, validating, and sharing learning limit our ability to tap the potential of personal learners.

Finally, alongside diversity and homogeneity run persistent equity gaps in education attainment that have links to the innovation constraints they create. The diversity/homogeneity paradox described above is useful for providing touchpoints on how colleges and universities would show up in an ecosystem and how they are likely to develop (or not) interdependent relationships with other stakeholders.

Yet there is hope in examples of post-secondary innovation from the past that provide further guidance to ecosystem formation. At various times in US history, social, economic, and political challenges created opportunities for policymakers, educators, and employers to catalyze institutional innovation in post-secondary education. The industrial revolution begat the land grant university movement (1860s), urbanization and factory economy growth begat the community college movement (1950s), and the advent of the knowledge economy begat the degree completion college movement (1970s).

These three examples are relevant because they demonstrate an attempt to meet the needs of a new group of learners and stakeholders in light of economic and social change. Importantly, these movements were complex, rooted in both national and regional economic and political realities, and manifested results at different paces. One nuanced note is that these movements created newer institutional forms and were less successful at ecosystem level interdependence though each was a step in the right direction. From them, we learn that ecosystems are messy, especially at first, and are often created as different stakeholders wrestle with the dissonance of competing expectations and outcomes desired. Only through this process does interdependence eventually take hold, and an ecosystem come into being.

A brief and more human-scale corollary to this historical snapshot of innovation in post-secondary education is to focus on adult learning in the colonial period and early industrial revolution. During the colonial period, mutual improvement clubs, apprenticeships, and agricultural societies provided opportunities for learning both the news of the day and more specific job-related skills. Moving into the early industrial revolution, evening schools associated with factories and, more independent, mechanics institutes formed as ways to teach technical skills. These examples are instructive for two reasons. The first is that they range from informal to more formal and structured in design for learning. So, the nation has always blended personal learning with more formal education. It is in our DNA. Second, many of these examples are built around small groups and cohorts on personal learning journeys together. These examples illustrate that large ecosystems are built from smaller relationships and interdependencies. An ecosystem that links personal learning and formal education may actually scale via smaller relationships and connections.

Based on the personal learning stories herein, it is clear that individuals seek knowledge for reasons far beyond employment. Yet work, employment, and economic mobility are important touchpoints for personal learners and, in fact, impact health, citizenship, and community involvement. Employers are both consumers and providers of learning. Based on research by the Georgetown Center for Education and the Workforce. US employers invest upwards of $500 Billion on formal and informal training, which includes tuition reimbursement. This amount dwarfs even the public investment in post-secondary education. This training investment represents a variety of purposes and formats which, to date, have struggled with a consistent way of measuring quality and impact on either the individual or the business.

Further, much of the investment goes to those that have already achieved post-secondary credentials, especially a bachelor's degree. This raises questions about how broadly human capital development is spread into the nation as a whole. Moreover, even with knowledge and learning, readily discussed as central to business success, training investment remains closely tied to relative labor market demand and business cycle change. These realities - different purposes, formats, quality control, and business cycles - all provide clues to the affordances necessary for an ecosystem that connects employers and post-secondary institutions to develop, function, and thrive. Affordances, adapted for this context, are the properties of learning experiences and tools that allow the personal learner the opportunity to adapt them to advance further along pathways in the ecosystem.

Questions help to frame affordances. What if we used more employer training dollars for employees with less than a bachelor's degree? How would this impact personal learning journeys? How would it impact the colleges in the ecosystem? What if employers aligned outcomes for workplace training with those of post-secondary education certificates in related disciplines? Would this create a better return on investment across stakeholders? Affordances are important because they point to a reality of an accurately conceived post-secondary education ecosystem – it is emergent, adaptive, and resilient. Thus, by definition, it is not easily planned or anticipated. Employers, indeed, all stakeholders must embrace this reality if true post-secondary ecosystems are to thrive.

The focus on colleges and employers is not meant to disparage all the other key stakeholders and the importance they play in the formation of a post-secondary education ecosystem that documents, validates, and shares all learning. Instead, they are used here as examples to frame ecosystem thinking and building such that sustainability, resilience, and adaptability result. With this in mind, I will turn to guiding themes adapted from years of writing and researching at the intersection of post-secondary education and personal learning journeys in the hopes they can help undergird the creation of successful ecosystems.

Guiding Themes for Promoting Ecosystem Emergence:

- **Learning is Continuous.** We are now in a learning society that requires that all learning – workplace, military, community, and college—be connected to optimize human capital for social mobility and economic competitiveness. All stakeholders—personal learners, colleges, employers, policymakers, community-based organizations—must be present to this reality and behave as if it is true.
- **Learning can be Connected**. Learning science, innovative pathways, and technology tools are making it possible to document, validate and share all learning from competencies to credits across many settings, including family, workplace, military, community, and college.
- **Context Matters.** Equivalent learning does not equate with successful portability across settings. Learners–whether a corporate employee, service member, boot camp participant, or online course taker–need to recognize their own knowledge, skills, and abilities in order to move across settings and, also, require support to continue learning in college or other environments.
- **Start Small, Scale Fast.** Personal learning and ecosystems are built from small interdependencies into larger ones. Smaller cohorts, pathways, and models such as those described in this text can be indicators of the interdependencies necessary for personal learning to plug into the ecosystem and add to its robustness and resilience.
- **Transparency and Incentives Matter.** Learners, employers, colleges, and other stakeholders all bring different perspectives to the understanding and purpose of evaluated learning. Transparency means all stakeholders have the same information about what has been learned and how it will be transferred to a college setting. Incentives mean that there are strong motivations for each stakeholder to optimize the transfer of learning across settings. Public policy, employer, and college policies and practices must align transparency and incentives.
- **A Technology Revolution is Needed.** Connecting learning remains a high-touch and nuanced human-centered exercise. Whether at the point of learning

from a life experience, evaluating a workplace training course, documenting that learning for sharing, or having it reviewed on a college campus, the processes that support credit for prior learning under-leveraged current technology. To scale this practice, we need to use artificial intelligence and data analysis to reduce costs and automate review while embracing open data standards and common definitions to increase portability.

- **Balance Speed, Diversity, and Quality.** Learning, technology, and a demand for skills in the labor market drive a reasonable impulse and urgency to connect all learning. Yet, we are still discovering much about how learning can be validated, documented, and shared across multiple life contexts. Thoughtful stakeholders will balance the speed at which the need to learn is emerging, the diversity of ways people are learning, and our ability to ensure the quality of learning and how it is interconnected.

These guideposts are deliberately broad. An emergent, resilient, and adaptable post-secondary education system that honors, validates, and shares human capital derived from personal learning is perforce organic, even as we attempt to harness it for societal impact.

Peter Smith has done us all a great service by linking the pursuit of personal learning with individual and societal transformation into a more equitable, inclusive, and just. He has posed a challenge to build an ecosystem that is both human and societal in scale and scope. We all need to get busy.

Appendix

UnderGround Programs – Emerging Pathways for Learning and Work

Each of the people featured in *Stories from the Educational Underground* ultimately found a way to achieve their goals. But doing so required that they create their own pathway through a wilderness of life challenges and, at best, vague directions as to where and how to access their dreams. Traditional higher education has fairly clear directions, signals, and rules. For most of these people, however, searching for their opportunity was like skiing in a blizzard without goggles.

As the new ecosystem emerges, including colleges as we know them today, its components and opportunities will be available and accessible to all on an ongoing basis throughout life. And good information, mentoring, networking, respect, and financial support routinely afforded people of privilege will be accessible to all. The organizing value of the ecosystem will be access to opportunity in learning and work in response to the needs of the learner throughout life.

Here are some of the pathways that, taken collectively, will comprise the new ecosystem.

New College Models

New ways of delivering post-secondary education are being created and expanding in America on a regular basis. New institutions and programs are being established while traditional colleges are developing online and low-residency options to respond to the new demands of learners and employers.

Alternative educational models, such as online and technologically-enhanced-education, were considered "radical" and "experimental" as recently as 20 years ago. So, they are not new in a literal sense of the word. Having said that, most alternative models did not exist as major options before the year 2010. And they have continued as growing, but "underground" activities until the last few years. The COVID-19 pandemic has catapulted the need for and the availability of new forms out of the closet of American higher education.

The variety of models available today—online, hybrid, self-paced, community-based, asynchronous, and others—are the opening act in a play that will see significant diversification in the years ahead. And the methods and practices employed in those models—intense advising and mentoring, assessment of prior learning, evidence-based assessments, open education resources, and learner self-direction, to name a few – will be increasingly flexible, learner-centered, and connected to tangible employment requirements. As the Presidents' Forum (*www.presidentsforum.org*) has said, the focus has to be on "Learners First."

As new educational institutions and models appear, it is critical to understand their quality and, therefore, their value. Regional accreditors, state agencies, and a national regulatory association, NC-SARA (*www.nc-sara.org*), perform these validations.

The institutions that participated in or were mentioned several times in this book's work all fall into this category. Their URLs are listed below.

> **College UnBound** (*www.collegeunbound.org*)
> **SV Academy** (*www.sv.academy.org*)
> **The Community College of Vermont** (*www.ccv.edu*)
> **Purdue Global University** (*www.purdueglobal.edu*)
> **University of Maryland Global Campus** (*www.umgc.edu*)
> **Western Governors University** (*www.wgu.edu*)
> **Colorado Technical University** (*www.coloradotech.edu*)
> **Bellevue University** (*www.bellevue.edu*)

Workplace-Based Models

There has been a dramatic change in the attitudes of many major employers over the last 10 years. Prior to the current period, in-service training was highly selective and targeted towards employees who were essential, highly placed, and/or long-term. The common theme was, "Why should I invest in people who might simply leave and take their value elsewhere?"

Today, that attitude has begun to change dramatically. Employers are reckoning with the high costs of turnover in the early months of employment coupled with low morale in their workforce due to low quality of work life. As a result, more attention is being paid to training during all phases of employment including, on-boarding and up-skilling. And, significantly, less concern is focused on the employee's longevity.

The programs that contributed interview subjects to *Stories from the Educational Underground* are strong examples, though not the only ones, of this positive change in employment practice. And Goodwill Industries, as a national non-profit is coming at the issue from a different perspective. All are offering and providing services differently, networking with colleges through third-party institutions such as CAEL. (*www.cael.org*) But the common denominator is significant subsidies and support provided by the employers for the workers who are enrolling.

Goodwill Industries (*www.goodwill.org/*)
The Goodwill® network, consisting of more than 150 independent local nonprofit organizations in the United States and Canada, with a presence in 12 other countries, has a history of adapting to labor market shifts and dynamic employer demand. The Goodwill Opportunity Accelerator incorporates field-proven and evidence-based solutions in every phase of career-focused workforce development services. The Goodwill Opportunity Accelerator is an agile framework designed for easy adoption and rapid adaptation in local communities. It promotes consistency and quality among the individual Goodwill organizations as service providers while facilitating rapid evidence and data-informed improvements for systems change. *www.goodwill.org<http://www.goodwill.org/>*

McDonald's Archways to Opportunity (*www.archwaystoopportunity.com*)
The *Archways to Opportunity*™ program from McDonald's enables restaurant employees to learn English language skills, earn a high school diploma, benefit from education and career advisors and receive upfront college tuition assistance up to $3,000 after just 90 days of employment. Since its inception in 2015, Archways to Opportunity has given out $90 million in tuition assistance and supported 50,000 restaurant employees. Archways to Careers is available to employees at McDonald's U.S. restaurants and franchisees. For more information about McDonald's support of education, please visit *http://www.mcdonald's.com/people.*

Walmart - Live Better U - (*https://walmart.guildeducation.com/partner*)
Walmart's website on the program with an overview of their investment in their associates *https://one.walmart.com/content/usone/en_us/company/news/popular-content/education-articles/unlock-the-future-introducing-live-better-u.html*

Amazon Career Choice Program (*https://amazoncareerchoice.com/home*)
(*https://www.aboutamazon.com/culture/upskilling2025*)

Bridging Services

Another new form of organization is the bridging service. These organizations act as value-enhancing go-betweens between colleges and universities and other organizations and individuals. Qualified bridging services save colleges and universities the costs and complications of developing the software and organizational expertise to compete in these emerging markets.

So, where Guild Education primarily links corporations to colleges for the purpose of employee training and education, StraighterLine works with both individuals and institutions to smooth the transition to college with pre-approved courses and credits. In both cases, the beneficiaries include adult learners who want to get employment rewards as well as academic payoff.

Credly provides a different type of service, offering lifelong portfolio services for the accumulation of formal and informal learning. They work primarily with digital credentials, connecting learners with employers, training providers, and associations. And having a connection to accredited college and university programs is part of the package as well. Again, these services and relationships help pave the way for adult learner/workers.

Other examples of exceptional bridging services include College Promise and Year Up.

> **StraighterLine** (*www.straighterline.com*)
> *https://www.edsurge.com/news/2021-01-11-how-this-company-is-helping-to-solve-some-of-higher-ed-s-thorniest-challenges*
>
> **Credly** (*www.credly.com*)
> Credly is helping the world speak a common language about people's knowledge, skills, and abilities. The company was founded in 2012 to help people connect their verified abilities to career opportunities through what was emerging technology at the time: digital credentials. Now, Credly operates the world's largest and most connected digital credentialing network. As of 2021, tens of millions of credentials have been earned and are managed on Credly, and more than half a million digital credentials are shared by earners each month.
>
> **Guild** (*www.guildeducation.com*)
> Guild's platform provides access to a custom network of nonprofit universities and learning providers, a range of educational programs, tuition payment management, and end-to-end coaching support.
>
> **Year Up** (*www.yearup.org*)
> Year Up is committed to ensuring equitable access to economic opportunity, education, and justice for all young adults—no matter their background, income, or zip code. Employers face a growing need for talent while millions are left disconnected from the economic mainstream. These inequities only further perpetuate the Opportunity Divide that exists in our country—a divide that Year Up is determined and positioned to close.
>
> **College Promise** (*www.collegepromise.org*)
> College Promise is a national, non-partisan, non-profit initiative that builds broad public support for funding the first two or more years of postsecondary education for hard-working students and ensuring those students have access to quality educational opportunities and supports.

Validation of Personal Learning – Giving Credit Where Credit Is Due

The importance, value, and power of validating personal learning runs as a consistent theme throughout *Stories from the Educational Underground.* Currently, there are basically four different approaches to validating personal and experiential learning.

- CAEL (*www.cael.org*) has made its name over almost 50 years on the high-quality assessment of experiential learning through portfolio development.
- That model has expanded over time to include the evaluation of courses that happen outside of college for college credit by a respected and reliable third party. The American Council of Education (*www.ace.org*) has been a leader in this model for decades.
- Some bridging services, like Straighterline (*www.straighterline.org*), use their "all you can eat" subscription tuition policy to allow the learner to go directly to the examination that certifies creditworthiness and take it. If the individual passes the exam without taking the course, then credit is awarded and transferred to the partner college.
- And institutions, such as Western Governors University (*www.wgu.edu*), University of Maryland Global Campus (*www.umgc.edu*) and College UnBound (*www.cu.org*), incorporate validated personal learning into the satisfaction of their course and evidence requirements for academic progress in a blended model.
- *Cashing In: How to Get Real Value from Your Lifelong Learning,* Huggins and Smith. (Dubuque, Ia: Kendall Hunt Publishing, 2013) is a workbook to assist assessment of prior learning.

A GPS for Learning and Work

The GPS for learning and work is the service which ultimately gives the learner and the employer control over their careers and decisions. It is, to use the President's Forum phrase, the ultimate "Learner First" service. (*www.presidentsforum.org*)

Every new car and mobile phone have an increasingly sophisticated GPS travel application that tells you how to get from where you are to your destination of the day in the most efficient and direct way. Of course, if you decide to take a more scenic route, there are always the second and third options offered. Whichever route you choose, however, you are secure in knowing that the information, the directions, and the estimated time to destination is essentially accurate and dependable.

The same kind of flexibility and focus is coming to educational planning, career preparation, and job placement. Whether you are an independent learner, an adult looking for the right college, a first-time job seeker, someone unemployed or under-employed, or a career-switcher, The GPS will support your quest.

The GPS will be free, non-profit, independently managed, and algorithmically-driven to assure dependability and accuracy. And it will allow the learner to do the following things as s/he builds and renews the learning path that fits her profile and aspirations throughout life.

- Identify any existing gap between current knowledge, skills, abilities, and behaviors and those required for a specific career or job classification, including licensing and required tests.
- Identify resources—programs, institutions, employers, other - that are available to help fill that gap, including costs, proximity, scheduling, and time requirements.
- Deliver specific information on jobs—current availability, location, pay scales, and alternatives that are close to the original request.
- Clarify the extent to which the program or institution in question will recognize and accept your personal and experiential learning.
- Store your learning record and allow it to be updated at will.

The GPS will be easily accessible to the individual via cell phone and computers and available to be used by third-party practitioners, including high school guidance counselors and career advisors as they serve their learners.

Early innovators in this critical space include the following.

- **eMSI** (*www.emsi.org*)
- **Burning Glass** (*www.burningglass.org*)
- **The Open Skills Network** (*www.osn.org*)
- **Strada** (*www.strada.org*)

These five areas and these practitioners are only selected examples. They represent the beginning of the long-term trend to create a lifelong, publicly accessible integrated ecosystem for learning and work.

References and Citations

Introduction

Carnevale, Anthony; Schmidt, Peter; Strohl, Jeff. *The Merit Myth: How Our Colleges Favor the Rich and Divide America.* New York, New York: The New Press, 2020.

Lohr, Steve, "Up to 30 million in U.S. Have the Skills to Earn 70% More, Researchers Say." *New York Times*, December 3, 2020.

Rose, Todd. *The End of Average: Unlocking Our Potential by Embracing What Makes Us Different.* New York, New York: HarperOne, 2016.

Smith, Peter. *Harnessing America's Wasted Talent.* Hoboken, New Jersey: Jossey-Bass, 2010.

The Center for Creative Leadership. www.ccl.org. Accessed 2016.

Weisse, Michelle. *Long Life Learning.* Hoboken, New Jersey: Wiley, 2021.

Section One

Hilton, James. *Goodbye Mr. Chips.* Boston: Little, Brown, 1934.

Section Four

Adolphs, Ralph and Anderson, David. *The Neuroscience of Emotions.* Princeton, New Jersey: Princeton University Press, 2018.

Conclusion

Eliot, T.S. *Little Gidding.* London, England: Faber and Faber, 1942.

Rios, Alberto. excerpt from "A House Called Tomorrow" from Not Go Away Is My Name. Copyright © 2018, 2020 by Alberto Ríos. Reprinted with the permission of The Permissions Company, LLC on behalf of Copper Canyon Press, coppercanyonpress.org.

Smith, Peter. *Free-Range Learning in the Digital Age: The Coming Revolution in College Career, and Education.* New York: SelectBooks, 2018.

CPSIA information can be obtained
at www.ICGtesting.com
Printed in the USA
LVHW100237290821
696364LV00002B/3